Humor From The Country

by storyteller and historian
Jerry Apps
photos by Steve Apps

The
Guest
Cottage Inc.
dba Amherst Press

The Guest Cottage Inc. dba Amherst Press
Minocqua, Wisconsin

The Guest Cottage, Inc.
dba Amherst Press
9587 Country Club Road
PO Box 1341
Minocqua, WI 54548

Library of Congress Cataloging-in-Publication Data

Apps, Jerold W. 1934-
    Humor from the country / by storyteller and historian Jerry Apps;
photos by Steve Apps.-- 1st ed.
    p. cm.
    ISBN 1-930596-00-6 (alk. paper)
    1. Chain O' Lakes Region (Wis.)--Social life and customs. 2. Apps,
Jerold W., 1934---Childhood and youth. 3. Farm life--Wisconsin--Chain
O'Lakes Region. 4. Chain O'Lakes Region (Wis.)--Biography. I. Apps,
Steve. II. Title.
F587.W3 A55   2001
977.5'98--dc21
2001000819

Printed in the United States of America
Layout and design by Camin Potts
Editing by Nancy Root Miller
Marketed by The Guest Cottage, Inc.

Dedication

*To my grandchildren,
Josh, Ben, Christian,
and Nicholas—
may they listen, laugh,
remember the stories,
and pass them on.*

Books by Jerry Apps

The Land Still Lives

Barns of Wisconsin

Mills of Wisconsin and the Midwest

Breweries of Wisconsin

One-Room Country Schools: History and Recollections From Wisconsin*

Rural Wisdom: Time-Honored Values of the Midwest*

The Wisconsin Traveler's Companion

Cheese: The Making of a Wisconsin Tradition*

When Chores Were Done: Boyhood Stories*

Symbols: Viewing a Rural Past*

*Published by Amherst Press

Contents

Part I: Country Ways

Part II: Stories

Part III: Farm Talk

Acknowledgments

The storytellers I have known over the years, many of them my relatives and others neighbors in our central Wisconsin rural community, have influenced me greatly. I especially want to thank my twin brothers, Darrel and Donald Apps, who reminded me of and added details to several stories included in this book. Donald was also especially helpful in spotting potential photographs—many of which appear on these pages.

Steve Apps, Staff Photographer with the *Wisconsin State Journal* and my son, took all the photos for this book and also made critical comments on much of the manuscript. Sue Apps Horman, my daughter, commented on several stories, and made many suggestions for improvement. My wife, Ruth, as always, read the manuscript several times, searching for problems large and small—and finding them, too. Nancy Root Miller, an editor who has worked on several of my books, did her usual excellent job of spotting omissions, oversights and dumb mistakes. A special thanks to Roberta and Chuck Spanbauer, former owners of Amherst Press, for their encouragement, support and willingness to put my ideas and stories into print. Their helpfulness will not be forgotten. And finally, sincere thanks to Nancy Ravanelli and her staff at the new Amherst Press for their support and interest in this project.

Rural Humor

Rural humor included practical jokes ranging from smearing Limburger cheese on the muffler of the newlyweds' car, to stuffing rocks in grain bags so that the fellow carrying the grain from the threshing machine to the granary walked with a staggering gait and a look that said, "I've never carried such heavy grain."

Humor could also be more subtle: the way a fellow wore his cap, how farmers greeted each other, and the nicknames they used. Often you didn't learn a fellow's real name, or its correct spelling, until he died and his obituary appeared in the newspaper. Pinky Eserhut was Alvin. Stub Davis was Harold. Morty Elephant was really Mortimer Oliphant.

Rural humor also included "putting one over" on an urban relative, such as telling a four-year-old city cousin that potato bugs were strawberries and that he should pick them and eat them. Giving elaborate directions to a lost city soul when he needed only to travel a mile, turn right and he would be back on the highway. Leaving a city-bred salesman to cower in his car while the farm dog stood by the car door barking. "If the guy is that afraid of old Fanny, he deserves to sit."

Country folk also had a language of their own. To those new to the country, the way rural people talked was seen as quaint and strange and often downright funny. The language of the country was not funny to those who lived there; it was the way they communicated and often a way to use fewer words to convey more complicated messages. For instance, "neck of the woods" meant where you lived, "woodpecker thaw" referred to a warm spell in February, and "no power in it" was how mushy store-bought bread was described.

Every neighborhood had at least one story-teller, someone who was able to take everyday, ordinary events and weave them into a tale that sent people into spasms of knee-slapping laughter. Most of these storytellers stayed close to the facts, embellishing here and there, especially as time passed and the story was repeated. They spun stories about bad weather, ornery cows, runaway horses and bumbling salesmen. They put a humorous twist on what, at the time, had seemed like a calamitous situation—a straw stack that caught on fire, a pickup truck that tipped over, a mad bull that charged its owner. They usually started with "Have you heard…?" or "Do you remember when…?"

Most rural communities also had at least one person who invented facts that became the stuff of outrageous tales. These community truth-stretchers told of monstrous trees, gigantic fish, mighty horses, Herculean men, catastrophic weather, and much more. They were despised by some—"You can't believe a word Amos says"—and loved by others who knew what they heard wasn't so but enjoyed hearing it anyway.

In addition to the storytellers of various stripes, every rural community had one or more people who did atrocious, idiotic things that no clear-thinking person would do. And they kept doing them, providing constant comedy to those watching their antics: a fellow who planted strawberries under a big oak tree because he wanted to pick berries while in the shade; a guy who planted watermelons on a side hill because he said they would all roll down into the valley when they were ripe.

At least one neighbor was good with one-liners, had a head full of them, and was able to spit them out when asked and often when he wasn't. "Don't buy a horse that is blind in one eye and can't see out of the other." "In winter it's too cold and in summer there's not enough time."

Humor allowed country people to live through the tough times, when the rains didn't come and the crops dried up, when a favorite cow died, when milk prices fell, and when someone in the family was injured. Country humor was homemade; it was of the people, and usually without the aid of outsiders. As the family farm and rural neighborhoods disappear, we are losing humor that was so important to everyone who lived in a rural area. For country people, good weather nourished their crops; humor nourished their souls.

PART I
Country Ways

Beyond the Books

Book learning was supposed to improve farming, and in some ways it did. But there were many things that a farmer needed to know that never found their way into a book. No one ever wrote about how to:

- Shovel dirt, shovel oats, fork cob corn into a crib higher than your head, and pitch cow manure into a manure spreader.

- Shock oats, shock corn, and pile hay into bunches that don't tip over with the slightest breeze.

- Pick corn by hand.

- Plant potatoes with a hand planter.

- Pound nails into dried white oak boards without bending the nails.

- Saw boards straight enough so that when they are nailed together the gap isn't obvious.

- Fork hay with a three-tine fork, pitch straw, fork cornstalks that slip this way and that, and pitch oat bundles into a threshing machine (the trick is to stick the fork just above the twine that binds the bundle).

- Milk cows by hand.

- Dig potatoes with a six-tine fork for ten hours at a stretch.

- Teach a calf to drink and not complain (too much) when you end up with a milk bath.

- Call cows—yelling loud enough so the cows will hear in the back forty, which may be a couple miles from the house. (This takes practice, but saves many hikes on a hot afternoon or a drippy, dewy morning.)

⧗ Chop off chicken heads cleanly, decisively, without any qualms about dying chickens dancing around headless.

⧗ Harness a draft horse that is so big you have to stand on a box to get the hames over the horse collar, and risk the big beast's pushing you against the side of the stall and squashing you like a horsefly.

⧗ Cultivate corn with a one-horse cultivator.

⧗ Splice a hay fork rope that breaks just when you are unloading the next-to-last load of hay and a thunderstorm is coming up in the west.

⧗ Sharpen a knife so it will cut paper and shave the hair off your arm.

⧗ Stretch the new barbed wire fence you and Pa strung across the pasture south of the barn tight enough so it doesn't sag in the hollows and not so tight that it breaks with the first staple you pound in place.

⧗ Notch a tree with an ax.

⧗ Use a crosscut saw so it doesn't pinch.

⧗ Start a fire in the kitchen stove that keeps burning after you leave for the barn in the morning.

⧗ Walk in the woods so quietly that wild game doesn't hear you.

⧗ Read the evening sky and predict the next day's weather—accurately, because the threshing crew is coming in the morning.

⧗ Figure the total in your head when the salesman says he'll give you two bucks a bushel for the potatoes in your cellar and you know you've got 356 bushels or thereabouts depending on how many rotten ones you find.

⧗ Console your six-year-old son when a horse steps on his favorite kitty and kills it.

⧗ Tell your wife that she'll have to wait another year before you can fix up her kitchen when she knows you are putting running water in the barn this fall.

⧗ Measure distances by walking and counting your steps.

⧗ Estimate the acreage in a field just by looking at it.

⧗ Set fence posts in a straight line by sighting from one to another.

⧗ Know when grain is ready to harvest by sight and feel.

⧗ Get your kids up in the morning to help with the chores.

⧗ Keep on the good side of all your neighbors even when, deep down, you can't stand at least one of them.

⧗ Keep your mouth shut when your neighbor does something dumb. The neighbor will usually learn his mistake without your help.

⧗ Compliment your wife on her skills in milking cows, forking manure, and feeding calves. Even though she may be less competent than you'd prefer, you couldn't do the work without her.

⧗ Praise your farm dog. A dog will do anything for its master with a little praise.

⧗ Learn to appreciate all kinds of weather, the good and the bad. Neither hangs around long enough for you to get used to it.

⧗ Keep your negative comments to yourself when eating at your neighbors' and the cooking is not near as good as you get at home.

⧗ Be careful what you say about your neighbor's wife, good or bad. Both kinds of comments can get you into trouble.

The Farmer's Cap

Farmer's caps, almost all of them baseball type, come in an assortment of colors—dark green, brown, yellow, tan, blaze orange, purple, white—and most of them advertise something. Farmer's caps advertise seed and feed companies, implement dealers, tractors, chemical companies and more. Most farmers get their caps as premiums for buying a certain seed corn, for test-driving an expensive new tractor, or simply for showing up at a chemical company's booth at the county fair.

A farmer's cap has multiple uses beyond advertising products, such as keeping the sun off a bald head and shading eyes on hot summer days. How a farmer wears his hat can make a statement.

Straight and even, pulled down to the ears: A practical fellow who doesn't want to lose his cap to a gust of wind

Tipped toward one ear: A bit of a show-off, cocky.

Pushed back with the bill high on the forehead: Friendly, easy to talk with. (Or it may be a cloudy day and the fellow merely wants to see better.)

Pulled down low so the eyes peer out from under: Doesn't want to be bothered. "I mind my business, you mind yours."

Crooked on the head, the bill slightly off to the side: Fellow doesn't have a wife to tell him, "Emil, straighten your cap. It looks dumb the way you got it."

How and when a farmer removes his cap tells you a lot.

 Farmer yanks off his cap and slaps it against his knee: He heard something funny. Or he's trying to remove dust from it.

 Farmer yanks off his cap and throws it on the ground: The guy is mad. Don't say anything more to him.

 Farmer and his wife are in an expensive restaurant and he doesn't want anything to happen to his cap. He carefully removes it and places it on the chair beside him. People with expensive hats will leave them in the cloakroom. *(But not the farmer who has a free cap with a picture of a John Deere tractor on the front. "Heard people steal caps like this," the farmer says.)*

Rules for Country Kids

When I was growing up on a farm, we had several rules, most of them unspoken. My brothers and I knew what they were; we also knew the consequences if we broke them. The rules included:

- Don't talk back to Pa or Ma.

- Don't leave food on your plate.

- Don't talk with your mouth full.

- Don't belch at the table.

- Don't spill your milk.

- Don't take the last piece of bread, the last piece of chicken, the last anything.

- When offered seconds, refuse—the first time.

- Don't leave the table until everyone has finished eating.

- Take off your cap when you come into the house.

- Leave your dirty boots on the porch.

- Don't tattle.

- Never cuss, or if you do, make sure Ma can't hear.

- Don't listen in on party-line phone conversations.

- Always wear clean underwear to town.

- Don't whistle when you can't think of anything else to do.

- Never start a fight you can't finish.

- Learn to run fast—a good way to avoid fights.

- Never make fun of someone who is different from you—especially if he is bigger.

- Don't complain about going to church; it doesn't do any good.

- If the teacher punishes you at school, expect a more severe punishment when you get home.

- Don't speak unless spoken to.

- Comb your hair when you go to school.

- Don't shoot holes in the barn roof.

- Keep at least one blade of your jackknife sharp.

- Don't walk behind a horse that is tied without first speaking to it.

- If a horse's ears are laid back, watch out. He's ready to either bite you or kick you, depending on where you are standing.

- Don't try to break up two dogs fighting.

- Never let a cat into the house.

- Do not make a pet of a pig; it will destroy your taste for bacon.

- Never turn your back on a billy goat.

- No matter how difficult the job, don't complain.

- Do more than is expected of you.

- Don't climb the windmill.

- Don't tell the neighbors what happens at home.

By Way of Greeting

By nature rural people are friendly, most of them anyway, and they greet everyone, folks they know and those they don't. The form of the greeting will vary, however. Here are some examples:

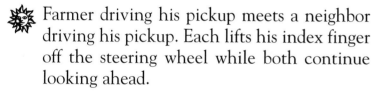 Farmer driving his pickup meets a neighbor driving his pickup. Each lifts his index finger off the steering wheel while both continue looking ahead.

Farmer driving his pickup meets a stranger in a pickup. The farmer will lift his index finger off the steering wheel, but will look to see if he may have seen the other driver before.

Farmer driving his pickup on a country road meets a stranger driving a fancy new car. Farmer lifts his left hand off the steering wheel as he passes. Looks to see who would be driving such a fancy car and almost hits the ditch.

Farmer drives past a neighbor's place, sees no one in the yard, but waves anyway, just in case someone saw him drive past. He doesn't want his neighbor to think that he's stuck up.

Farmer walks into the feed store in the village. Meets an old friend coming out. Nods and says his name, usually a nickname: "Shorty," "Junior," "Red," "Slim," "Stub," "Billy," "Arnie," and continues walking.

City Meets Country

After World War II, people from the cities began sifting into rural communities, buying land for summer homes, buying farms and taking up farming, or simply coming to spend their summer vacations. Even though rural people resisted the changes suggested by their new city neighbors, the changes nonetheless occurred. Here are a few:

🏠 Communities with quaint, long-standing names such as Skunk's Hollow and Pine Snake Hill became Pleasant Valley and Pine Tree Knoll.

🏠 The North Road, so called for years, now has a sign and a new name, Apache Drive. Apparently no one bothered to figure out that no Apache Indians had ever set foot in the area.

🏠 Shorty Davis, who cusses regularly, drinks too much and chews tobacco, is now described as "colorful."

🏠 Several deer, busy mowing off a farmer's cornfield and sworn at by the farmer, are described by his new city neighbor as "nature's creatures" that are merely following their instincts.

🏠 During the summer months, when city visitors are many, a small sign appears in the window of the drive-in restaurant: "If you want fast service, go back to the city."

🏠 Fred Everson, the laziest man in the village, is now described as "interesting."

A comment overheard at the gas station: "Do you know they don't even have garbage pickup out here?"

George Evans, known by all the natives as the biggest liar in town, is now referred to as a "rural storyteller."

As long as many folks can remember, there has been a stop sign at the corner of Highway 22 and Main Street in the county seat. Now there is a stoplight.

Saturday night was always town night, with stores open until nine. Now the stores close on Saturdays at six, and every day is shopping day, or so it seems.

The Town Chairman has begun getting comments that farmers who spread manure on their fields create quite a smell. Shorty Davis said, "Too bad these folks didn't take a whiff of cow manure [he used another word] before they moved out here."

A new, unspoken rule at the grocery store: Lines at the checkout counter should move right along. No stopping to ask about the clerk's son who has been sick, or to comment about the weather.

A new question comes up at the town meeting: "When do you plan to widen and blacktop some of these dusty country roads?"

A comment overhead at the grocery store: "They said it was quiet, but some animal kept me awake all night." (Some folks just don't appreciate whippoorwills.)

PART II
Stories

TOWN OF AURORA
W2171

TOWN OF AURORA
W2175

Cold Winter

No matter what direction a north wind comes from, it always blows cold.

It was Saturday night in late February and the men had gathered around the potbellied stove in back of Hotz's Hardware while their womenfolk shopped for groceries. The group included Walter Bowen, Milton Jones, Bill Miller, Arlin Handrich, Norman Mueller, Griff Davis, Pa, myself and maybe one or two more.

Talk was about the winter, how it had dragged on without so much as a woodpecker thaw, how the snow had piled up and the frost had gone down. Walter Bowen offered that he had snow piled as high as his woodshed. Griff Davis said he had a tunnel that connected his house to the barn and that he'd shoveled the snow about as high as he was able. "I don't know what I'll do if we get another storm like the one last week," he said.

"Yup, a bad winter," Pa offered. He was usually not one to top what the previous person said. But well he could have, because I knew the snow in our farmyard came clear up to the kitchen roof in one place, where the wind had blown it around. The snow along the road had drifted so high you had to duck to go under the telephone wires. I wanted to say all this and nearly opened my mouth at one point, but Pa gave me one of those looks that meant I'd better keep my mouth shut.

With snow depth pretty well covered, talk turned to frozen ground. Somebody remembered that in the 1930s, the frost had gone down more than five feet in some places, even more where the wind blew the ground bare. Someone inquired about frost depth this year. Everyone sitting around the stove knew it could vary from almost none where the snow had piled deep on the east or south side of some building, to several feet deep on a snow-free hill.

"Talked with Jake Smith the other day," Milton Jones said. "He digs graves, you know, and has a good fix on frost depth. Jake told me he couldn't remember when there was more frost in the graveyard, down nearly six feet."

Everyone shook their heads and made a few "um"s and "you don't say"s. "Jake said this cold weather keeps up he'll have to quit grave diggin' until spring," Milton offered.

> *The winters used to be so cold that when a man cussed, the words froze and you didn't hear them until the following spring.*

I piped up with the obvious question. "What'll happen to the dead bodies?"

There was a little ripple of laughter around the cheery red stove, an "everyone knows the answer to that question" kind of laugh. But I could tell by the look on some of the men's faces that they were wondering, too. What do you do with a dead person if you can't bury him?

Arlin Handrich had the answer. "They just put the body in cold storage until spring and do the buryin' then. They do that up north all the time. Some springs the grave diggers and the undertakers are beyond themselves busy to move all the bodies in the ground before they thaw out."

"There's something else to worry about, too," Norman Mueller said. Norman hadn't more than grunted and offered a few "yup"s during the conversation so far.

"And what might that be?" Pa asked, taking

the bait. Everyone knew Norman's truth-stretching ability and wondered what was coming.

"Fellow up north, a woodcutter he was, walked ten miles to town, bellied up to the bar at the Wolf Paw Tavern, drank for a couple hours and fell off the barstool, dead. Far as anybody knew, he had no kin. The ground was froze so deep they couldn't bury him, so they wrapped him in an old blanket and laid him on a shelf in a unheated shed out back the tavern. They knew he'd keep there 'til spring.

"Well, it started warmin' up some in late April and the snow started goin'. The bartender at the Wolf Paw remembered the dead woodcutter he'd earlier stashed in his shed and figured he'd go have a look to make sure he was all right."

I think it was Griff Davis who blurted out, "What could go wrong with a dead man stashed away in a closed shed?"

"Funniest thing," Norman continued. "The bartender remembered exactly where he'd put the body. What he found was only the blanket he'd wrapped around the guy. Then he opened the outside door and there he saw fresh man tracks leading away from the shed in the mushy snow, heading off toward the river and out of town."

"You don't say," Walter Bowen offered.

"Gospel truth," Norman said. "Told the story just like I heard it. Stashin' a body in cold storage can have some strange results."

"Time to go," Pa said. He got up and I followed him to the door. Outside Hotz's Hardware, I asked Pa, "Could that have happened? Could someone have been frozen half the winter, wake up and just walk away?"

"You know Norman," Pa said. But Pa never answered my question.

Norman Mueller

Fellow was a man of few words.
When he spoke folks believed that even fewer words would have been better.

There were occasions in our community when times were hard and things weren't going right. Everyone became solemn. Complaining replaced laughter. Sullenness crowded out smiles. When this happened, a good storyteller could lift a community's spirits, even when the person was known to stretch the truth a little. Norman Mueller was such a person. He was short, had a full head of red hair and most of the time a day-old growth of red whiskers. He always wore wide red suspenders and a belt which stretched over his ample midsection. Norman, one of our closest neighbors, lived just down the road from our farm and he stopped by often.

He was well known in the neighborhood for his ability to tell a story, but not everyone liked his tales, especially those who were sticklers for the truth. Ma was one. She said Norman never told the truth in his life, wouldn't know the truth if he stepped in it. Pa was more forgiving; he said that Norman sometimes stretched the truth a little, but that he surely knew how to tell a story.

Some neighbors thought that Pa was way too generous in accepting Norman's lying. Allen Davis said Norman stretched the truth way beyond breaking it. John Macijeski believed Norman created a new kind of truth that never existed, except in his head. I liked Norman and I think a lot of other people did too, even those who complained about his truth stretching. Norman's voice traveled up and down and was full of expression as he spun a story. I liked to hear him laugh, too. He shook all over and his face got even redder than it naturally was.

Norman had as many problems as the rest of us, but you'd never know it by talking to him. I recall a rainy day in fall, when Norman pulled into our yard, turned off the engine in his 1938 Dodge and scampered to the house, his head down against the driving rain, water dripping from his old felt hat. He no more than got comfortable in the chair by the kitchen stove when he began one of his tales; at least I figured that's where his talk was headed.

"Say, Herm," Norman said to Pa. A grin spread across his red face. "You hear what happened to Charlie George?"

"Nope."

> *Every farm task is difficult until you discover the art of it, from splitting wood to hoeing potatoes.*

"His team ran away."

"When?"

"Last week, when he was in town with his grist. You know Charlie. A little slipshod sometimes."

"Yup."

"Well, he didn't tie up his team good enough and they got loose and ran all the way home with the wagon, leaving poor old Charlie behind."

"You don't say," Pa answered.

"Well, by the time Charlie found somebody to give him a lift home, the team was out of sight, galloping down the north road."

"Break anything?"

"Didn't break nothin', but something worse happened."

"It did?" I could see that Pa was becoming curious about where the story was headed. I surely was listening carefully.

"Well, that team of Charlie's got going so fast that they het up the wheel bearings on the wagon so the hubs caught fire."

"Is that right?" Pa said. He tried to keep a serious look on his face.

"Gospel truth as I sit here by your stove on this rainy day in October." Norman always said "gospel truth" when he was in the middle of telling a tall tale.

"Charlie finally got a ride with Allen Davis in his Model A Ford. It took them nearly an hour to get home. Know why?"

"Can't say as I do," Pa said, a hint of a smile teasing his lips.

"Well, that wagon with its hubs ablaze set little fires all along the road. Old Charlie and Allen had to stop to put out each one."

"You don't say," Pa said.

"That's how it happened, gospel truth. Funniest thing. Can't you just picture those guys beating out all them little fires, tryin' to keep 'em from spreadin'?" Norman began laughing. So did Pa. Norman's face was as red as sunset. I laughed too, even though I figured there wasn't a shred of truth in the whole story.

But that afternoon, as we sat next to our kitchen stove watching the cold fall rain splatter against the windows, our spirits lifted. Pa was laughing, I was laughing, and I even heard Ma, who was standing by the sink, giggling.

Olaf and Oscar

When cultivating corn with a tractor, keep one eye on the corn row,
one eye on the cultivator, one eye looking out for stones
and one eye on the fence at the end of the field.

Those who didn't know them well figured they were bachelor brothers. They weren't. Olaf Johansen was Oscar's father. The wife and mother had been dead for years. The two looked alike and the differences in their ages didn't show that much. Both were tall and thin with hollow cheeks and quiet gray eyes. You never saw either of them without at least a week's growth of scraggly whiskers. They wore identical blue denim overalls and barn jackets, in both cases so spattered with cow manure that you didn't want to get real close to them for fear some would drop off on you. That's to say nothing of the smell, especially on a hot summer day. If you happened to be somewhere, say at the Mercantile in town, and you smelled cow manure, nine times out of ten one of the Johansens was nearby.

Aside from appearance (and smell), Olaf and Oscar were farmers that everyone looked up to, or perhaps better said, looked down upon. For instance, when it came to planting their crops, Olaf and Oscar were always late. Even an average farmer knew that if you wanted a crop that amounted to anything, you planted it on time. You stuck oats in the ground in April, same thing for potatoes. Corn you planted in May. Corn was kind of fussy. If you planted it too early there was a good chance a late frost would take care of it

25

and you'd have to replant it. If you waited very long into June, best you could hope for was a few nubbins or some frozen cobs that weren't near ripe come fall and would rot in the crib.

While Pa and Bill Miller and the Macijeski brothers usually planted their crops first, Olaf and Oscar were always last. When we were planting corn, they were still hauling manure from the huge, steamy pile in front of their barn. We'd hauled manure back in April.

Here is where Olaf and Oscar came in handy. You knew that if you planted oats when they did, it was too late. Same thing for potatoes, corn and all the other crops. They were the "too late measuring stick," and nobody, absolutely nobody, in the neighborhood wanted to be known as having planted their crops after Olaf and Oscar.

People would talk about it at the gristmill, at the hardware store, and at the cheese factory. "Did you hear that Johnny Johnson didn't plant his corn until after the Johansens?" It was like hearing that you were lazy, or didn't milk your cows on time, didn't take your wife to church on Easter morning, or didn't have much of a wood-pile behind your house.

As you might guess, the Johansens were also last when it came to harvesting. We'd have tucked the last load of hay into the haymow while Olaf and Oscar were just starting to cut hay. All the neighbors would have their corn in the corncribs, and Olaf and Oscar's corn was standing out in the cornfield in shocks. Usually, winter arrived before they got around to dragging the corn shocks onto the barn floor where the two men sat, day after day in the cold, shucking ear corn out of the dried, frozen stalks. Sometimes, if an early, heavy snow came—which was not unusual—you'd see Olaf and Oscar in the cornfield with a team and wagon, chopping the corn shocks free with axes. It was a terrible job, cold and miserable. Olaf

> *Never make a mistake, but learn from those that you do make.*

and Oscar never changed, never speeded up their operations, either on the planting or the harvesting end.

Even though farmers in the neighborhood made fun of them and talked about them often, deep down every farmer was glad they were there.

They were the neighborhood standard for inferiority. Most neighborhoods have a few, maybe one or two, farmers who tend to do most things right. They become standards of comparison for doing a good job. But to keep everything in perspective, a neighborhood needs at least one farmer on the other end of the scale. One who does everything wrong. With both ends of the spectrum identified, you can decide where you fit without too much effort.

If Olaf and Oscar ever moved away, then someone else would end up on the bottom of the heap and become the standard for neighborhood inferiority. Nobody wanted to be saddled with that possibility.

The Watkins Man

An old horse, an old dog and an old farmer have much in common:
they are slow but wise.

He stopped by our farm at least once a month. I don't think I ever heard his name; we simply called him the Watkins man. He was a frail little fellow, scarcely as tall as Ma, with a chalky white face, long skinny fingers and thick glasses that slid down his nose when he talked. He always wore a necktie, even on blistering hot days in summer when no one wore neckties, not even to church.

He came the second week of every month. Ma dreaded his coming because he took up a lot of time with his sales pitch—and it was always the same. Ma once said she hoped he'd change his talk some, but he never did. She never complained to him, though, and never hid in the closet when his car pulled into the yard. Some of the neighbor women did that—they ran and hid and let the poor Watkins man pound on the door and hoped he believed that no one was home, even though he could see food cooking on the stove.

My brothers and I liked his visits. We liked what he had to say and most of all we liked it when he began spreading Watkins products all across the kitchen table. We even enjoyed watching Ma fidget when the time dragged on and he didn't leave. I remember one time when Ma was canning green beans and she caught a glimpse of the Watkins man's car pulling into the yard. He drove a dark green Plymouth.

"It's that goll-darn Watkins man," Ma said. She was probably thinking stronger words, but she was not one to curse. My brothers and I were helping with the beans, cutting them into small pieces so she could stuff them into jars and boil them on the stove.

"Wish he'd picked another day," Ma said, brushing a loose strand of hair out of her face and retying her apron.

Fanny barked a couple times and ran up to the car, wagging her tail. She looked forward to the Watkins man because he always talked to her, patted her on the head and even called her by name.

Soon he was on the porch, pounding on the door. "Watkins man," he called out. He carried a black leather case in his left hand.

Ma went to the door. "Mrs. Apps, how are you?" he said. He was always polite and friendly, different from some of the salesmen who stopped by and didn't seem to care who you were and how you felt.

He sat his black display case on a kitchen chair, unbuckled the strap that held it together at the top, and pushed his glasses back on his nose. Opening the case was what I liked best, for in it were all the popular products the Watkins man sold. As he did on every visit, he began taking bottles, boxes and tins out of the case.

"How's your supply of vanilla, Mrs. Apps?" he asked. He set a big bottle on the table. I read the label: "Watkins Double Strength Vanilla Extract." A cork was stuffed into the bottle's opening.

"Here," he said. "Have a whiff of this." He uncorked the bottle and handed it to me. It smelled good. My brothers each smelled the open bottle and then Ma did, too.

"Good, huh?" the Watkins man said.

"Don't need any vanilla," Ma said.

"How about liniment, how you fixed for liniment? You know it's good for about everything. Use it on a lame horse, put it on your sore back, even pour a little in a glass of water and it'll calm an upset stomach. Want a smell?"

"No," Ma said. "I know how liniment smells."

"Can I leave a bottle with you?"

"Don't need any liniment," Ma said.

"How about salve? Good for cows' udders, good for your hands, too. Makes 'em all soft and nice. You get a little cut, well, it keeps infection out."

"Don't like the smell," Ma said.

"Does smell a little," said the Watkins man. "But if it smells, then you know it's good. That weak-smellin' salve you buy just ain't got any power in it."

"Don't need any salve," Ma said.

"How about cinnamon, you got enough cinnamon? Goes good on rice pudding, good on sweet rolls. Tops off sweet rolls real good."

"Don't need any cinnamon," Ma said. "Do you have any pepper?" I could see that Ma wished the Watkins man would pack up his boxes and bottles and tins and be on his way so she could get back to canning green beans.

"Sure I got pepper, the best pepper anywhere around." He took an immense can of pepper out of his case and set it on the table along with the vanilla, liniment, salve and cinnamon.

"You got a smaller box?"

"Yup," he said. He pulled out a drawer near the bottom of his case and took out a little can of pepper.

"How much is it?"

"A quarter."

The Watkins man packed up his samples while Ma went to the cigar box on the clock shelf in the dining room, where she kept her egg money.

The Watkins man put the money in his pocket, grabbed up his black case, said thank you and closed the screen door slowly so it wouldn't bang.

Ma put the box on the shelf in the cupboard, along with four other little unopened boxes of pepper.

Nancy and the Drinking Cup

If you must sing, do it when you're after the cows.
Cows don't care if you can't carry a tune.

Nancy was a good cow. She gave her share of milk, took her stall in the barn without need of encouragement and was generally easy to live with. What we didn't know about Nancy was that she was stuck in her ways. She did what she did, and she didn't want to do anything differently.

Pa and I didn't really know this about Nancy until he decided to put running water in the barn. (As was true on many farms, we had running water in the barn twenty years before we had it in the house.)

The installation took a couple days, with plumbers running a pipe from the pump house to the covered stock tank in the haymow and installing individual drinking cups by each cow stall. To get a drink, a cow needed only to push her nose down on a flap in the cup and it would fill with water.

Before, the only source of water was an outside stock tank. No matter how cold a winter day, the cattle were hustled outside for water. Just keeping the stock tank from freezing was a major effort. Pa kept a wood-fired tank heater going in the stock tank to keep away the ice. With plumbing inside the barn, the cows could stay in their comfortable stalls, no matter how miserable the weather outside.

33

Pa asked one of the installers how we should teach the cows to use the new drinking cups.

"Let 'em get a little thirsty," he replied. "They learn how to use these cups real fast when they need a drink."

By that evening, the cows were becoming restless. Several were bellowing their discomfort and announcing that they wanted to be turned outside to visit the stock tank. Nancy especially let out a long pitiful "mooooo" that was designed to send shudders of sympathy up and down your spine.

Pa and I worked our way down the aisle in front of the cows, pushing down each metal flap and filling each cup with water. Soon the cows were getting the idea that by pushing down the flap themselves, they could get water. All except Nancy. Either she played dumb, really was dumb, or she was simply an uncooperative beast that wanted nothing to do with anything different or new. She'd only drink when

> *Look down when walking in a cow pasture.*

one of us pushed the flap for her. When her drinking cup was empty, she'd let out a mournful "moo" and we'd push down the flap again.

Pa figured when she was thirsty enough she'd nose down the flap by herself. Little did we expect what would happen. When Pa and I opened the barn door the following morning, it was quiet. No mooing.

"Guess they've all learned how to use the drinking cups," Pa said.

"Even Nancy?"

"Seems so," Pa replied. Then we saw it. What we didn't want to see. There was water in the aisle behind the cows, in the manger and several cows were standing in water.

Pa immediately suspected a loose connection to the stock tank in the haymow. But there was no loose connection. He and I carefully inspected the entire system for leaks and there were no leaks. Something had gone dramatically wrong, but what?

We walked in front of the cows, inspecting each of the drinking cups. Everything appeared as it should, until we came to Nancy's cup. It was filled and running over. We surmised that not only had Nancy learned how to use her drinking cup, but that she had struck on a way to sabotage the entire system. By holding down the flap in her drinking cup and not letting it up, water flowed all over the barn.

This was obviously Nancy's way of letting us know she wanted nothing to do with this new-fangled watering system. From that day, Pa stuck a stone under the flap of Nancy's drinking cup. He removed it each morning and evening so she could drink.

Weston Coombes

Happiness for a farmer is a barn roof that doesn't leak,
a pasture fence that is not broken, and a daylong rain in May.

"Good man, that Weston Coombes," Pa always said. The label had nothing to do with how he lived his life and everything to do with his ability for hard, physical work for hours on end. Weston could dig fence post holes like no man I had ever seen, one after the other, lining them up so they were straight and true. He dug potatoes with a six-tine fork so fast you had to hustle to keep up with him if your job was to pick the potatoes up. He snapped ripe corn off cornstalks so quickly that one of the neighbors claimed he could do it as well as a John Deere one-row mechanical corn picker.

I knew no man better with an ax or a crosscut saw. Weston was probably even better than Pa at woodcutting. He not only had the necessary skills, but he never stopped for a break unless you insisted that he did. Pa, after swinging an ax for a couple hours, insisted on resting for a few minutes. I was way down the rungs of ax and crosscut saw skills and off the ladder completely when it came to requiring breaks. Half an hour on the handle of a crosscut and I was ready to rest. Not Weston. When Weston finished sawing through a log, he was immediately looking around for the next one to cut. I was looking for a place to sit down.

Weston was short, about five foot five, and skinny. "Stand him sideways and he wouldn't even cast a shadow," Pa said.

Weston always had several days' growth of whiskers, and his shaggy hair looked like it had never known a comb and seldom saw a barber. His gray eyes were sunk back into his head and stared out of his long, thin face. He was the kind of guy that would scare the bejeebers out of you if you met him on a lonely road on a dark night.

He wore a well-worn mackinaw jacket and a black wool cap with fur-lined earflaps. The cap was stuck full of cow hair, a reminder that he wore the same cap for everything he did—probably the only one he owned.

Though skilled at farm labor, Weston was a gentle, soft-spoken man who never talked unless you spoke first. And then he'd only say a word or two.

"Nice snow we had last night, Weston."

"It was."

"Be a lot colder tonight, twenty below zero likely."

"It will."

It was tough carrying on a conversation with Weston. After a little while it seemed like you were doing most of the talking, which was in fact the case. This was likely a reason Weston got so much work done; he didn't waste any breath talking.

Weston had been subject to epileptic seizures and couldn't get a driver's license. Thus he either walked to our farm from his place—about two miles or so—or Pa fetched him with the Plymouth.

On this particular Saturday in January, Pa had picked up Weston right after breakfast and we spent the day sawing down trees and hauling logs up to the house with the team and bobsled. We'd later cut the logs into firewood. It was a cold day; the temperature never climbed much above zero and the woods were filled with three feet of snow. From my perspective, cutting wood under these circumstances was mean and miserable. I know Pa didn't care much for the job either, but he didn't say anything because we'd soon be out of wood. Not one word of complaint from Weston.

"Which tree you want, Herm?"

We'd scarcely gotten out into the woods and I was still catching my breath from walking in deep snow.

"How about that one?" Pa answered. Pa was as

out of breath as I was.

Immediately Weston began notching the designated oak with his ax.

Thwack, thwack. Wood chips flew.

Soon we were sawing and the tree was down and a pile of brush had accumulated off to the side of the tree trunk. I glanced up at the hazy sun, hoping that noon was near. But noon was a long way off; no sense in even asking Pa to check his pocket watch.

It was cold and getting colder. Pa pulled a small bottle of kerosene out of the sack where he kept a couple files for sharpening the axes and a wedge for pounding into a tree to keep the saw from pinching. He splashed the kerosene on the brush pile and tossed in a match. A flame flashed up and in a few minutes the brush pile was a place to warm hands and any other part of the body that was suffering. I couldn't pick out one part of my anatomy that wasn't freezing, so I just crowded up to the brush pile-turned-campfire as close as I could get without melting my five-buckle rubber boots or scorching my coat.

"Come over and warm up, Weston," Pa said.

Weston hadn't stopped working while Pa was starting the fire, and I was crowding up to it as close as I could get.

With the suggestion, Weston walked over to the fire, took off his leather mittens with their wool liners and rubbed his hands together. Frost had accumulated on the whiskers around his mouth.

I was only about half warmed when Weston pulled on his mittens, shouldered his ax and was back limbing the tree we'd just taken down.

"Good man, that Weston," Pa said, smiling.

"He is," I said, trying at least to mimic his speaking style. I knew I would never come close to matching his skills and his endurance.

"They don't make 'em like that anymore," Pa said.

"They don't," I answered, pulling on my leather mittens and grabbing up my ax.

Pa's Chariot

Walking behind a horse-drawn plow teaches you how to do many things at the same time: control the team, keep the plow in the ground, look out for stones, walk with one foot in the furrow, and enjoy the beauty of a spring day.

For several months Pa'd been thinking about a way to haul manure when the snow was too deep for the manure spreader to work. One day, when he was in the village, he struck up a conversation with Jim Colligan at his welding shop. Colligan was a handy man with a welding torch and could make just about anything out of used parts and a good idea.

And Pa had the idea. He began scratching out the design for a winter manure sled on the shop's dirt floor. Colligan watched carefully, rubbing a hand through his reddish hair.

He pushed back the steel-rimmed glasses on his nose and said, "Herm, that just might work. Yup, your idea just might work."

I helped Pa take apart the old bobsled that we'd stored in the back shed. Pa'd used the bobsled at one time to tote logs out of the woods. It had massive wooden runners, two pairs of them, and reminded me a little of the sled I used for sliding downhill, but it was many times bigger and made entirely of oak, except for the steel strips on the bottom of the runners. The runners were about six feet long, ten inches high and three inches wide, and they were turned up in front to enable them to glide through deep snow.

I helped Pa toss the runners into the back of the pickup and we were off to the village and

Colligan's welding shop. Pa drove staring straight ahead, both hands on the steering wheel, not saying anything. When he had his mind on some new idea, he didn't stray off it for a minute.

"That ought to do it," Colligan said when he saw the bobsled runners. "I've rustled up some other stuff for a manure box. We'll leave the back end of the box open so when you lift it, everything will slide out on the ground."

In a couple weeks, Colligan phoned to tell us the invention was finished. What he actually said was, "Herm, your chariot is done." From that moment on, all who heard about it knew Pa's invention as Herm's chariot. Colligan had passed the word around the village about what he was making, and several farmers had stopped by with the thought that they might have manure-toting chariots made for them. But to a man, they said they wanted to see how this one worked before they'd have a chariot made.

It was quite a machine. All painted green, it stood up high in Colligan's welding shop. Colligan had fashioned a handle to the front of the box that you pulled to tip the chariot box and dump the contents. But for it to dump properly, it had to be high off the ground. As a result, the chariot was a little on the unstable order.

"Don't go driving on any side hills, Herm, or you'll tip this thing over."

"I can see that," Pa said as he walked around the old bobsled, admiring Colligan's work.

"Fine-looking chariot," Pa said after one time around it.

"It is that," Jim Colligan said.

Pa hired Ross Caves, the local trucker, to haul the machine out to the farm. As soon as Ross unloaded it, Pa harnessed the team. The horses shied a little when Pa hitched them to the chariot, but soon he was standing in the box with the horses' leather lines in his hands. He said "giddap" to the team and they were off.

The horses trotted with their heads high, the snow flying when their hooves struck the ground.

> *Don't compare your work with that of others. Some will do better; some will do worse.*

The runners of the chariot made a two-ribbon track where they plowed through the snow in the little field just south of the barn.

"It's gonna be all right," Pa said. "Gonna work just fine. Make manure hauling a lot easier."

That night it snowed more than a foot, with a strong wind.

"Looks like today is the day," Pa said, smiling. "Give that chariot a trial run." It wasn't often that Pa was happy on a snowy day.

We pitched the chariot box full of fresh cow manure. Pa climbed on back and he and the team were off to the far field. Unfortunately, there was no place for the driver to stand, except in the manure. But Pa had six-buckle overboots and didn't seem to mind.

In a short while, he was back with the team and an empty chariot.

"How'd it go?" I asked, while I helped him unhitch the team and lead them into the barn.

"Went fine. Just fine. No problems. Gotta let Colligan know how well this thing works."

The next day was a different story. Pa didn't come back and didn't come back, and when he finally did, he was walking behind the team. There was no chariot in sight.

"What happened?" I asked.

Pa was covered with manure from the top of his wool cap to the tip of his overboots.

"Chariot tipped over," he said. His face was red and his glasses were crooked on his nose. "Should have stayed off the side hill."

With a log chain and the team, we got the chariot back on its runners. Because of the soft snow, there was no damage.

The next day, Pa came back from the field all excited. "Spotted a jackrabbit sitting in the fence row," he said. "I'm going back with the twelve-gauge and see if I can bag him."

A while later, I heard the shotgun's blast coming from the field and I figured Pa would be bringing home a rabbit. I waited and waited. No Pa, no chariot, no rabbit. When he did appear, he was sawing on the lines of the horses and they were at

> *Nothing grows without roots.*

a gallop, the chariot bouncing along the snow-packed road.

"Whoa, whoa," Pa yelled when he arrived at the barn.

"Horses seem wild," I said, patting Frank on the shoulder. He was still skittish and shaking.

"Team ran away," Pa said. "I found the rabbit under a little bush, held the lines between my legs and fired the shotgun. Well that gun no more than went off and the team lit out a-runnin'. I fell down in the back of the chariot, but managed to hold onto the lines. Every time I tried to get up, I slipped and fell in the cow manure left in the chariot when I'd dumped it. I drove 'em around and around that twenty-acre field three times before they calmed down enough so I could drive 'em home. Ain't all that calm yet."

I couldn't keep from laughing. Once more Pa was covered with cow manure, even worse than when he'd tipped over.

Next time we were in the village, Colligan asked how the chariot was working out. "Fine, just fine," Pa said. Pa also told him about his adventures tipping over and shooting jackrabbits. Colligan was laughing so hard he had to hold his side. Not one farmer asked Colligan to make a manure chariot once they'd heard about Pa's escapades.

Mad Hog in a Straw Stack

The grass may be greener on the other side of the fence,
but it doesn't matter if you're not able to climb over.

Bill Miller was our closest neighbor to the south, about a half-mile away. His barn needed painting so he hired Johnny Evans to paint the high places that tended to make Bill a little dizzy and unsure of himself. The painting went well for the first couple days, with Bill working on the low ladder and Johnny hitting the high spots. On the third day they had worked around to the north end of the barn, which was closest to the straw stack. Bill had threshed a few days earlier so the stack was fresh and tall, enough straw to bed his cattle throughout the winter and provide a cozy shelter for his hogs. Bill had built a little pig house, which was buried under the straw stack. A tunnel led to the outside.

Painting on the end of the barn proceeded well. Johnny had the thirty-two-foot wooden extension ladder extended to its full height, and he still had to reach well over his head to paint the barn peak.

Without any announcement, Johnny started scurrying down the ladder, faster than Bill had ever seen him move. Ordinarily, Johnny was on the slow order.

"There's a hornet's nest up there," Johnny announced. "It's the biggest dang hornet's nest I ever seen. I got a rule. I ain't paintin' where there's hornets."

"We'll take care of them hornets," Bill said. "We gotta paint the peak. What'll people think?"

"They'll think there was a hornet's nest there, that's what they'll think," Johnny offered.

Bill laughed. He disappeared into the pump house and came back carrying a broken ax handle, an old shirt, and a kerosene can. He tied the shirt around the handle, doused it with kerosene and said, "Take this up the ladder with you and when you get close to the hornets, light it with a match. You got matches, don'tcha?"

"Yeah, I got matches. You sure this idea's gonna work?"

"It'll work just fine. One thing hornets don't like is fire. Be careful up there with the flame, though. Don't want you burnin' down the barn. Just light the shirt and poke it against the hornet's nest and then come on back down."

Johnny commenced to crawl up the long wooden ladder slowly and deliberately, with one eye on the steps and the other on the hornet's nest that seemed to grow larger with each step he took.

If you must hurry,
do it slowly.

"You sure this is gonna work?" he yelled down.

"Just keep goin', you're almost there. Remember, light the shirt just before you get to the nest and then touch the nest with the flame and come on back down. It always works," Bill reassured him.

Johnny continued climbing, more slowly now as he could see the hornets buzzing around the nest—hundreds of them, each with a stinger that seemed a foot long, just waiting to drill into his neck and arms.

When he got as close as he dared, Johnny wrapped the arm holding the ax handle around a rung of the ladder and reached into his pocket for a match with the other hand. He struck the match against the side of the ladder and touched the flame to the kerosene-drenched shirt, which immediately burst into a smoky, hot fire. Wasting no time, he climbed up a couple steps and touched the hornet's nest with the torch. Dead hornets began dropping on his arms, on his head and on his shoulders. Live ones angrily buzzed around his

head. But the smoke, at least for the moment, kept them away from him.

He must have thrust the homemade torch too hard against the hornet's nest, however, for the fiery shirt came loose and began floating downward toward the freshly threshed straw pile.

Without the smoke and flames as deterrents, the remaining hornets took after Johnny, who immediately began descending the ladder two steps at a time, yelling each time he believed a hornet had stung him.

Bill Miller's prize sow pig wandered under the ladder as the burning shirt floated downward. With perfect timing and extreme bad luck, the burning shirt landed on the back of the sow pig. The pig let out a loud grunt and ran into the tunnel under the straw stack, a perfectly natural thing, for the house under the stack was her home.

The situation had turned serious. Johnny was yelling to the top of his lungs, "I'm stung! I'm stung!" as he flew down the ladder. But much worse, the sow pig, with a burning shirt on her back, was under the straw stack. "Oof, oof," she grunted as she ran.

Quickly, Bill got on his hands and knees and followed the sow pig along the pig-high tunnel, through the smoke and into the depths of the pig shelter. The tunnel was dark and the smoke burned his eyes. Bill knew somewhere up ahead was a very mad sow pig and a smoldering fire that would engulf the entire straw stack, the barn and probably all the buildings in the farmstead.

Then he heard a few loud grunts and realized the sow had had enough of the smoke and heat and was headed back outside. There was no room in the tunnel for both pig and man, so Bill covered his head and the enraged sow ran right over his back and on to the outside.

Bill continued further into the tunnel. In the dark he found the smoldering shirt; the fire had gone out. With eyes watering, he dragged the smoking shirt with him to the outside, where he met both Johnny and the sow pig. Both had

> *First done often not best done.*

calmed down considerably. Neither was saying anything.

Johnny had only been stung twice, the sow pig's burns were superficial, and Bill was only a little sore from the sow's trip over his back.

"Guess I can finish the painting," Johnny said as he started back up the ladder.

Cloverine Salve

Don't buy a horse that is blind in one eye and can't see out of the other.

How could a kid resist? Especially when all he had to do was sell a few tins of salve. "White Cloverine Salve," the ad read. "Win a BB Gun or a Bicycle."

I tried to convince Ma that here was a good idea. Send no money and the company would mail twelve tins of salve to be sold for twenty-five cents each. All I had to do was walk around the neighborhood and sell this outstanding product that soothed chapped hands, relieved minor burns and helped heal cuts and bruises.

Ma was skeptical. She said that most people bought their salve from the Watkins man and they didn't need some fancy stuff that came in a little white tin with a picture of a clover on the cover. And besides, twenty-five cents was a lot of money for a small can of the stuff, no matter how great it was. I showed Ma pictures of the BB gun, jackknife, the bike and the other important equipment that was available for prizes.

"Look at this," I said. "All I gotta do is sell forty-eight tins and the BB gun is mine."

"Don't have to send in any money?" Ma inquired. She was baking bread and the smells of fresh bakery hung deliciously heavy in the kitchen. She had just opened the oven door for a peek at the six loaves that had turned a mouth-watering brown.

"Nope. You send in the money after you sell the salve. Says so right here." I tried to show her the ad while she was brushing butter on the tops of the bread loaves.

"I suppose it'd be all right," she finally said as she closed the oven door. "Wouldn't hurt to have some salve that didn't smell like disinfectant."

"Says Cloverine salve smells like clover." I said.

"We'll see."

A few days later the rural mail carrier delivered my package of salve to our mailbox. I ran up the driveway to the house with it and tore off the wrappings when I got into the kitchen. Here were the twelve tins of salve as promised. The cans were a little smaller than I expected and I had to smell deeply to come up with a hint of clover. But it was there. I pointed this out to Ma who took one sniff and said she couldn't smell clover. I said she should take a bigger whiff, but she said she was too busy to stand around smelling salve. She also reminded me the size of the cans was a tad on the small order, especially when they were supposed to sell for a quarter.

All of this was rather discouraging as I set out to make my rounds selling salve and earning a new BB gun. I thought I would start with Allen Davis. He and Kathryn always bought Christmas seals from me, usually only five cents' worth, but they always bought something. They lived about a mile south of our farm. From Allen and Kathryn's place I thought I'd take the half-mile trail through the woods that connected the Davis farm with the Hudziak place. Joe Hudziak's would be the second stop, and then on down the road for another three-quarters of a mile and I would be to Handrich's place and on to the Griff Davis farm a quarter mile or so further on.

I had it all calculated out. If I'd sell two or three tins of salve at each place, I'd have my BB gun in a few weeks. I skipped down the dusty road.

Kathryn Davis answered the door when I rapped. "What can I do for you, Jerry?" she asked, motioning me inside their kitchen.

"You wouldn't want to buy some white

Cloverine salve?" I said, holding up a tin so she could see the attractive cover with the green clover.

"I'll have to ask Pa," she said. Kathryn had continued to take care of the housework after her mother died several years ago.

"Pa, Jerry's here," she said in a little louder voice. Allen came in from the dining room.

"How's your Ma and Pa?" he inquired by way of greeting.

"They're fine," I said. I lifted up a tin of salve. "You wouldn't want to buy one of these, would you?"

Allen laughed. "Got lots of salve around here."

"But this salve smells like clover and it's good for chapped hands and cuts and stuff."

"'Spect so," Allen said. "But the salve I use on the cows and horses works just fine. Sit down. Let's talk for a spell. Haven't seen you for a while."

Ordinarily I enjoyed talking with Allen and Kathryn for an hour or so; they were always interested in what I was doing, what the twins were up to, how our cows were milking, whether we were having any troubles with our horses. That sort of thing.

In a little while Kathryn brought out some sugar cookies and some hot chocolate and the talk continued. I couldn't think of a way to leave without being impolite, even though I could see salve sales being pushed into the future.

Before I'd even thought about it, most of the afternoon had slipped away. I had an enjoyable time and at one point had almost forgotten that I was supposed to be selling salve and not eating cookies, drinking hot chocolate and shooting the breeze. I headed on home, just in time to start my chores.

"How'd the selling go?" Ma asked.

"Not very good," I answered. I didn't want to go into detail about how I'd gotten hung up at Allen and Kathryn's eating cookies and drinking

> *Fellow in town had a chance to sign up for a lifetime membership. He refused, said he didn't think he'd live that long.*

hot chocolate and hadn't sold anything.

"Maybe it'll go better tomorrow," she said.

The next day wasn't much different, although Mrs. Hudziak did buy one tin of salve. She said she'd heard about Cloverine salve somewhere and had wanted to buy some. "Couldn't find it at the drugstore in town," she said. She went on to tell me how glad she was I'd stopped by and then she fished a quarter out of the cigar box that stood on the counter in the kitchen and handed me the money. I gave her a tin of salve and said I thought she'd like it. She said she knew she would.

Things were looking up. Selling the remaining eleven tins would be a breeze. Except Mrs. Handrich didn't want any salve and neither did Griff Davis. I was back to feeling sorry for myself and wondering what I'd do with the remaining tins.

I told Ma about my one sale and several turndowns. She said I should save a tin for her. No trouble, I thought. Looked like right now I'd have

eleven tins for her. But I didn't want to tell her that.

That night Uncle Wilbur stopped by and he bought a tin. So did Aunt Louise when I saw her on Sunday, and likewise Aunt Arvilla. I shifted my sales tactics to work on relatives. I decided they'd buy salve as long as I didn't try to push too much off on them.

Ma said, "Stick to selling only one tin at a time." And that's what I did. I sold one more tin to a neighbor; I think it was Mrs. Rapp. I'd polished my sales approach so that I was bragging about the salve rather than approaching people and saying, "You don't want to buy any of this, do you?" Most of them said no before I had a chance to tell them how wonderful it was.

For love or money I just couldn't get rid of the last four tins of my first twelve. My thoughts of a BB gun or a new bike had slipped away. Now I was concerned about paying my bill to the Cloverine

> *When you are eating an apple and find a worm, be thankful it isn't half a worm.*

Salve Company. Ma helped me figure out that if I sent in all the money I had taken in so far with the sale of eight cans, I would be free and clear.

For a long time four tins of White Cloverine salve sat on the clock shelf in the dining room. I hoped that when someone stopped by they'd inquire what those four little tins with the clover design on the cover were. No one ever did.

Snoopy the Adventurer

Realize that your farm dog knows more about herding cows than you do.

I could tell she wasn't an ordinary cow when she and her partner walked down the ramp of Ross Caves' cattle truck. She blinked her big brown eyes a couple times and then looked around before she walked through the barnyard gate. She and her partner were Jerseys, with fawn-colored coats, dished black faces, and black horns that curved toward the front. Compared to our Holsteins, these Jerseys were little, something like Shetland ponies standing next to a team of Belgian draft horses.

Pa said he bought them to bring up our milk test. The creamery paid for milk based on its butterfat content. Holsteins were notorious for having low-testing milk, sometimes around three percent butterfat or even lower. Jersey milk, on the other hand, often tested more than five percent. Unfortunately, while a Holstein could fill a sixteen-quart pail at milking, a Jersey would scarcely cover the bottom. That was of course an exaggeration, but it was how Pa talked about Jersey cows. I was surprised to see them in our barnyard, even though they were a pretty sight.

After Ross Caves had left, Pa, the twins and I stood leaning on the barnyard fence, looking at our two new cows. "I think we'll name that one Louise," Pa said. He pointed at the larger of the two Jerseys that was off in the corner of the barnyard, eating grass.

"What about that smaller one, what should we call her?"

Pa had no more than asked the question when the little Jersey got down on her knees, stretched her neck under the barnyard fence and wrapped her tongue around some alfalfa that was on the other side.

"How about calling her Snoopy?" I suggested. And Snoopy it was. Louise and Snoopy, two Jersey cows with different personalities and different ways of behaving.

It wasn't long before Snoopy took over the cowherd. When the cows came home for milking, Snoopy was in the lead, walking with her head up and her tail swinging. The remainder of the herd walked behind in single file. Sometimes Louise, the other Jersey, was at the rear, sometimes in the middle. But there was never any doubt of Snoopy's position—she was the leader. Fanny, our farm dog, walked at the end of the long line of cows that stretched up the lane to the pasture. It was a sight to see: a little Jersey cow in front, a collie dog at the rear, and a collection of big, gangly Holsteins (and another Jersey) in the middle.

Early on, Fanny and Snoopy came to terms with each other. I don't know how cows and dogs communicate, but it's clear that they do. This was especially true with Fanny and Snoopy. Sometimes I saw them in the barnyard "talking" to each other. They would stand nose-to-nose. There was no barking or mooing, but it was clear a conversation was talking place. Ultimately, Fanny was in charge. It was clear that Snoopy had a strong personality, and I was surprised she didn't challenge Fanny. But she never did.

> *If a dog were a rooster, it would crow.*

It may seem like Snoopy was an ideal cow to have around, and in many ways she was. She took her place in the barn without fuss. She was easy to milk and she gave more than a bottom covering. Within a month, Pa noticed that the herd's milk test average had climbed a little.

But, alas, Snoopy had a dark side. We should have guessed as much from that first day in the barnyard when she stuck her neck under the fence. One morning a couple weeks after Louise and Snoopy arrived, Bill Miller phoned. "Say, Herm, you got a Jersey cow?"

"I do," Pa answered. "In fact, got two of 'em. Bringing up the test." Bill Miller had Holsteins, too, and understood.

"One of those little Jerseys is in my cornfield," Bill said.

"Must have busted the fence," Pa said. "I'll get right at it."

Pa and I tossed a couple of new fence posts, a post hole digger and a roll of wire into the back of the old Ford pickup and bounced across the dry pasture to where the fence separated it from Miller's cornfield.

Sure enough, there was Snoopy, up to her back in corn plants. She saw us coming but didn't stop eating.

"Get outta there, Snoopy," Pa yelled. He was hoping she'd leave the cornfield through the same hole in the fence where she entered. But there was no hole. Snoopy slowly walked down into a hollow, where the bottom wire of the four-strand wire fence was a little further off the ground. Without even looking at us, she knelt down and crawled under the fence. She proudly walked away.

"Well, I'll be danged," Pa said. "You see that?"

"I did," I answered.

"Never saw a cow do that before."

> *When you can't jump over it, go around it.*

Pa and I spent the next half-hour stringing another wire lower down, so no cow, not even a Jersey, could crawl under.

Two days later the phone rang again. It was Bill Miller and the Jersey was in his cornfield.

"How could that be?" Pa said when Ma gave him the message.

We returned Snoopy to the home pasture and spent the rest of the day fixing places where this inquisitive little cow could crawl under the fence. The phone calls continued. We didn't see her do it, but Bill Miller claimed he saw her leap over the fence. Pa was fast losing his patience with Snoopy, who continued leading the herd to and from pasture and giving rich milk, and was still the subject of many comments when visitors came by. "Isn't that a beautiful little cow." "What a beautiful animal, it must be such a pleasure having such a fine animal around."

Give a horse its head and it will always go home.

I heard all of this and so did Pa. He usually just grunted and shook his head in apparent agreement. I knew he wanted to blurt out that for all her good qualities, she had become a real problem.

Pa stopped by Hotz's Hardware and inquired about a cowpoke, which is a metal device that slips over a cow's head. It has hooks on the top and bottom so that when a cow pushes her head through or under a wire fence, the hook on the poke catches. A sharp prong pokes into the cow's neck when the hook makes contact, the idea being that a jab in the neck should change a cow's mind. A cow wearing one looks a little like she has an oblong metal picture frame over her head. A poke surely doesn't add to the appearance of an animal, except in a kind of comical way. Snoopy, when she wore the poke, had a melancholy look on her face. She walked with her head down and her tail limp.

For two weeks she stayed in the pasture. Pa declared victory and even took the criticism from those who expressed disbelief that a farmer would subject a beautiful animal to such inhumane treatment. Actually, the poke didn't harm a cow at all unless she tried to push her head through a wire fence.

Then the phone calls returned and we searched for Snoopy in Miller's cornfield. Three times she successfully removed the poke from her head before jumping over, crawling through, or sneaking under the wire fence. Pa was beside himself. I wondered what he would try next. Whatever it was, Snoopy always won.

Sometimes Pa took drastic action when he faced a problem he couldn't solve, and he usually made up his mind without telling anyone what he was going to do.

Every few weeks doing the summer, cow dealers came by the farm looking for cattle to buy.

"Got anything for sale, Herm?" one especially obnoxious dealer asked Pa one day. I knew Pa didn't like this fellow and sometimes commented that he was as crooked as a snake. Pa had never sold him anything before, but today he said quietly, "Yup."

"Whatcha got?"

"That Jersey cow over there."

"Good-lookin' cow," the dealer offered.

"Good test, too."

"Why you sellin' her?"

"Don't look right havin' a Jersey among all these Holsteins." Pa hoped that Louise would stay on the other side of the barn where the dealer couldn't see her.

"Good reason," the dealer said. "Good reason."

Pa and the dealer wrangled some on price and then agreed on a number. The next day

> *It is hard to get from here to there if you're unclear about here and haven't thought much about there.*

Ross Caves drove into the yard and backed up to the barn. Just as she did when she arrived, Snoopy walked up the ramp into the truck with her head high and her tail swinging. She had pride.

Fanny watched the goings-on. She barked once when Caves started the truck engine. Fanny stood at the top of the driveway, looking down the road long after the sound of the truck disappeared and the dust had settled.

FOR SALE

FARMALL

1939 FARMALL H
Pulling tractor 50 HP
608-375-5614

Junior's Shiny Tractor

One summer was so hot the hens laid cooked eggs
and the cows gave pasteurized milk.

Junior Osinski had a green Oliver tractor that he bought brand-new and there was nothing he thought more of. He kept his tractor so shined that a person could see his face reflected off the hood. At the end of a day's plowing, disking or cultivating, Junior always took time to wipe off the dust and grime that had accumulated on the machine.

Junior became the talk of the neighborhood with his tractor that looked as shiny and new as the day he bought it. When we were threshing that summer, my brother Don and Marvin Miller, who was my brother's age, decided they would pull a trick on Junior and his shiny tractor. "After all, he's asking for it," my brother and Marvin reasoned.

We were threshing at Osinski's place and we'd all filed into the house for the noon meal. I noticed that Don and Marvin left the table a little early, but that wasn't unusual. Folks often got up and left before the rest finished their pie and coffee.

It was a warm day in late August, sunny but no hint of a breeze. A good day for threshing because the dust didn't fly and the straw stayed put when it was blown on the straw stack.

After dinner, we all gathered under a big maple tree, resting in the shade and spinning stories of other threshing days. Junior's shiny green Oliver stood off to the side, near one of the bundle wagons. He'd unhitched it from the wagon before dinner for some reason and now he needed help to re-hitch. Junior climbed on the seat of his shiny tractor while Pa held the tongue of the bundle wagon. Junior had no sooner pushed the starter button when a high-pitched whistle came from under the tractor's hood, followed by a huge cloud of black smoke that hung over the machine like a thundercloud.

Pa yelled, "It's gonna blow up!" He took a step backward and fell over the wagon tongue, so he crawled on his hands and knees away from the doomed machine. Meanwhile, Junior leaped off the tractor seat and ran for the maple tree, where everyone was now on their feet, watching the whistling, smoking tractor.

Junior had just made it under the tree when there was a loud "kaboom" and more black smoke.

> *Those who are prone to show off are usually those with little to brag about.*

"I think your tractor's a goner," Bill Miller said.

"We'd better find some water and put out the fire before it causes more damage," somebody else offered.

But there was no fire. And soon there was no more smoke. My brother Don and Marvin Miller stood with the rest of the onlookers, keeping serious, concerned looks on their faces.

Slowly, Junior walked toward his tractor.

"Be careful, Junior," Don yelled. "Might blow up again." He said it with a straight face.

Junior eased forward a step at a time. I could see that he was ready to sprint away if he heard or saw the first inkling of another blast. Pa stood off to the side, brushing straw and dirt from his overalls. He'd lost his straw hat when he fell over the tongue and was waiting for Junior to find out if it was safe before he retrieved it.

Junior walked slowly around his shiny tractor, which was a little smudged here and there from the black smoke. Then he snapped open the hood and found the remnants of a prank car bomb, the kind that newly married couples often found in their autos, the type that could be ordered from a catalog. The device did little damage other than make a lot of noise and create a huge cloud of black smoke.

"Damn car bomb," he said, pulling off the wires and throwing them on the ground in disgust.

Everybody under the maple began laughing, all except Junior, who was mad, and Pa, who was even madder.

"When we find out who did this, there's gonna be hell to pay," Pa said. He was red in the face and trying to keep his false teeth in place. Whenever he got excited, his teeth came loose.

But Pa didn't find out then. Neither did Junior, until years later when Don and Marvin confessed their deed. Junior laughed when he heard. Pa didn't.

Oliver Lowe

If you live in the country and don't know what you are doing,
rest assured that someone else does.

Oliver Lowe was a city guy. Someone said he had been a math teacher in Chicago and had graduated from a university. All of a sudden here he was, with his wife and a couple kids, living on the old Blair place and farming. He didn't look like a farmer. He was short and skinny. He had thin arms without any hint of muscles and he wore thick glasses. We wondered why a schooled man such as Oliver had wanted to milk cows, cultivate corn, bale hay, and make a lot less money than he did in Chicago. It didn't make any sense. We also discovered several things about Oliver Lowe that didn't fit our community. When the neighbors got together, talk often got around to Oliver and what

a strange duck he was. He was always trying something new. At least he figured it was new. Neighbors, Pa and me included, considered most of his ideas dumb, the kind of stuff a city guy would do.

Our neighborhood was skeptical of anything new, no matter who came up with the idea. When Pa put running water in the barn, some of the neighbors thought the idea didn't make sense and was just a way of pampering our cows. When Bill Witt bought an electric generator and a bank of batteries so he could put away his lanterns and lamps, neighbors thought he could have found a better use for his money.

71

Now here was Oliver Lowe trying new things. For instance, he baled a bunch of alfalfa hay that was grass green. Anybody who knows a lick about making hay knows that you let it dry for a while before you bale it. If you don't let it dry, it molds and rots and no animal will eat it, and if you pack it too tight into your barn, you'll burn the barn down with spontaneous combustion. Except Oliver didn't stack his wet hay bales in his barn; he packed them in a big hole he'd dug in the ground.

"I'm creating a new generation of silage," he said. In addition to having a head full of strange ideas, Oliver also talked "city." Nobody in our neighborhood used words like "creating" or "generation" when they were talking about silage or anything else.

We all heard about Oliver baling wet hay. We knew his baler broke down several times because it couldn't take the punishment. Then we kept track while he piled big, heavy bales in an immense hole in the ground.

Nobody said too much at this point, for there might be an outside chance that Oliver was on to something, and his experiment with high-moisture alfalfa bales just might work. The style of criticism in our neighborhood was to poke fun of new ideas when someone talked about them. Then if the person had enough gumption to actually try the idea, keep your mouth shut and wait to see what happens.

I remember Pa talking about when Bill Witt first put marl on the field in back of his barn and then planted alfalfa. Marl, which consists of snail shells and long-dead water creatures, was dredged from the bottom of a nearby lake and then hauled with a wagon and spread by hand on the field. It was a lot of work. The purpose of the marl, which was rich in calcium carbonate, was to raise the acid level of the soil so alfalfa would grow. Pa told how people had kidded Bill Witt that he was wasting his time. A year later, Bill had a beautiful green field of alfalfa growing in back of his barn and soon all the neighbors were hauling marl and growing alfalfa. Those who had led the kidding wished they hadn't shot off their mouths quite so much.

Now we were faced with Oliver Lowe and his

idea of a new "generation" of silage. A couple months went by. Pa heard that when Oliver took the cover off his underground silo a powerful smell of rotten hay emerged and floated off across the road. Every last spear of alfalfa had rotted and what was supposed to be an innovative silo had become an ordinary manure pile.

The word of this failure spread through the neighborhood about as fast as the information that the country schoolteacher had gotten in the family way. Another time, during a dry summer when the grasshoppers were especially plentiful, Oliver decided he'd try a new way to control these pesky plant-eating insects. He fastened a piece of tin on the back of the sickle bar on his mower, the part of the machine that does the cutting. On the bottom of the tin he attached an ordinary eaves trough the same length as the sickle bar. As he explained his invention to Pa and me he said, "See that piece of tin?"

> *No matter what happens on a farm, next year will always be better.*

"Yup," Pa replied. Times like this Pa didn't say much, but he listened and watched real careful.

"See that eaves trough?"

"Yup," Pa replied again.

I still hadn't a clue how this invention was supposed to work. What he was telling us any dummy with two eyes could already see.

"So how does it work?" I asked.

Pa gave me a "give him a chance to explain it" look. But I didn't back off. If this was a new invention, I wanted to know how it worked. I didn't need any detailed description of tin and eaves troughs.

"Well," Oliver continued. You could tell he was a man with extra education from the way he talked and how he explained things. He wanted to make sure we knew every little thing about what he was doing before he went on.

"You pour some kerosene in this eaves trough."

"Kerosene?" I asked quietly. I didn't want another look from Pa for asking a question I should have left alone.

"Yes, regular kerosene. The kind you use to start a fire. The kind you pour into your lanterns."

I knew all these uses for kerosene and more. I thought about the time that I'd gotten lice at school and Ma washed my head with the stuff. Sure took care of the lice. Also kept everybody away from me for a few days—I must have smelled like a kerosene can.

Pa had a kind of silly grin on his face, but he didn't say anything. I figured he'd already caught on to the theory of the invention.

"Now the way this device performs…" Oliver said.

Why didn't he just say, "the way this thing works," I thought.

"I drive the mower around the hayfield, cutting hay. When the sickle bar frightens a grasshopper, the insect strikes the piece of tin and is momentarily stunned. It falls into the kerosene and dies. What do you think, Herman?"

Otto Olson's farm was so hilly his cows had short legs on the uphill side.

"I'd have to see it work," Pa said. Pa was never one to rely on words alone to convince him of anything. He wanted to see the invention in action, to see what it could do in a hayfield.

"Fair enough," said Oliver. "I'll be back in a couple of minutes with the team and we'll see how it performs."

"That'll be fine," Pa said. We sat down under a big oak tree and waited for Oliver and his team of horses to appear. They did in a few minutes. We headed out to the alfalfa field just beyond Oliver's machine shed. Pa carried the kerosene can.

Once in the field, Oliver readied the mower for cutting and poured the eaves trough two-thirds full of kerosene.

He said "giddap," and the team stepped off with the mower clattering behind. He had a confident look on his face, a kind of "Thomas Edison, I've invented something important" look.

I could see plenty of grasshoppers in the field, so the invention could be easily tested. Pa and I walked some distance behind the mower, watching grasshoppers hop over the metal piece and occasionally hit it and disappear from view. I figured they must have struck the metal, dropped into the kerosene and died, like they were supposed to.

After cutting for a hundred yards or so, Oliver yelled "whoa," and the team stopped.

"How's it workin'?" Pa asked. It was the right question.

"Killed a grasshopper," Oliver said.

"Just one?"

"Unfortunately the rest escaped," Oliver reported.

"Why?" Pa asked.

"First bump I hit, the kerosene spilled. Have to do some more thinking about this invention.

Something wrong with the mathematics."

I knew that Oliver had taught mathematics but I didn't see what getting the numbers right had to do with spilling kerosene when you hit a bump. That seemed more like common sense than mathematics. I didn't say what I thought this time, though.

When some of the neighbors got together on Saturday night, in the back of Hotz's Hardware, the discussion got around to Oliver and his new ideas. Pa shared the story of the grasshopper killer and there was loud laughter. Of course the new silo came up again, too. More laughter.

It was Allen Davis who put a stop to the fun making. In all seriousness, Allen said "It ain't Oliver's fault that he's got so much education. One of these days he'll come up with something we'll wish we'd thought of."

Cellar Grapes

Rural people know all about their neighbors—at least they think they do.

The summer rains had come regularly and the wild grapes that grew on the fence alongside the woods hung heavy with lush purple fruit. One night at supper, Ma said, "We ought to bottle up some of them grapes and make us a grape drink."

My twin brothers and I picked about a bushel of grapes. They were small—wild grapes don't compare in size with tame ones—but they were plump, sweet, purple and ripe.

Ma knew exactly what to do. She instructed us to pull the grapes from their stems, and then she began stuffing them into bottles, the same bottles we had earlier used for homemade root beer. The tiny grapes slipped easily through the narrow bot-

tle necks. When each bottle was about two-thirds filled with grapes, she topped them off with warm water and Pa and I capped each bottle with the bottle capper.

"We'll store them in the cellar," Ma said. Our cellar was a dark and dreary place with a dirt floor, lots of cobwebs and no windows. Depending on the time of the year, it either smelled like fresh potatoes, onions, cabbage and rutabagas (fall), or it smelled dank and musty (early spring). On the rough-sawn oak shelves fastened to the west wall were jars of canned pork, beef and garden vegetables (peas, carrots, beans and beets) along with quart jars of strawberries, raspberries, cherries, pears and peaches, plus various kinds of jellies and jams (strawberry, grape, raspberry, plum) and pickles (dill, sweet-sour, beet and watermelon). Ma had done all this canning throughout the summer.

We found room for the two dozen bottles of grapes on the canning shelves and I forgot about them. I suspect Ma and Pa forgot about them, too, for I don't recall ever being asked to fetch a bottle.

About six weeks after we'd stored the grape-filled bottles, a loud noise awakened me in the night, a kind of muffled explosion. It didn't sound like a rat trap snapping shut. The occasional rat found its way into the cellar and Pa always set a trap for them. This was more of a Fourth of July sound, like a firecracker going off. Maybe something had tipped over somewhere in the house. I went back to sleep and thought no more about it.

Pa and Ma had heard the sound, too, and the following morning Pa lit the lantern and went down to the cellar to have a look. When he came

> *Call your mother.*

back up the steps he said, "One of them bottles of grapes blew up last night. Glass all over the place, and grapes, too."

"That's awful funny," Ma answered. She had a disbelieving look on her face. "Don't doubt what you said. But how'd it happen? Rat must have bumped into the bottle and tipped it over."

"Could be," Pa said. "But I don't think so. I think that bottle blew up."

"How come?"

"Don't know, but I'll fetch up a couple bottles and we'll see what's going on," Pa said.

Pa brought up three bottles and carefully set them on the kitchen table. They were dusty and covered with cobwebs. Ma searched out a bottle opener, grabbed up one of the bottles and snapped off the cap. Little bullet-like grapes shot out of the bottle like they'd had a charge of gunpowder behind them. They went flying by Ma's nose so fast she never saw them.

It was a comical sight but such a mess. Here stood Ma with the strangest look on her face. She was staring at the empty bottle while grapes and grape juice dripped down on her from the ceiling and splattered on the kitchen table.

Pa was standing off to the side, laughing his head off. I didn't know if I should laugh or run. But it was sure funny seeing Ma trying to think out what had happened.

"Where are them grapes comin' from?" she finally asked. She brushed her hand across her forehead, creating a purple smudge. She was a sight to see.

Ma glanced at the drippy ceiling and back at the empty bottle, and then she began laughing, too. Soon all five of us were scrubbing fermented grapes from the ceiling, from the walls, from the windows, from the floor. Smelly, squishy purple grapes were everywhere.

When we were through, Pa said, "We'd better fetch the rest of them bottles from the cellar before any more blow up." That's what we did, carefully and gently, like we were handling bombs, which we were.

Outside, we snapped the caps off each bottle, being careful to point them away from us. Released grapes shot thirty feet or more. Pa reminded us that we'd probably be tempted to shoot these wild grapes at each other. He stood there to make sure that we didn't.

The following summer, the wild grape crop was also plentiful. I asked Ma if the twins and I should gather up a bushel or so for her. She said, "No, think I'll let the birds have them this year." She had a hint of a smile on her lips.

Billy Goat Bob

Keep your eye on the doughnut and not on the hole.

Nobody seemed to know how Uncle Bud got himself a billy goat, but he did. Once he had it, he didn't know what to do with it, so he called Pa.

"I got this billy goat," Uncle Bud said.

"You got a what?" Pa exclaimed. It took more than a little to surprise Pa but word of Uncle Bud having a billy goat seemed to do it.

"His name is Bob."

"How'd you come onto a goat?" Pa asked.

"Just got him the other day and I can't keep him here." Uncle Bud and my Aunt Arvilla lived in town, on a small patch of ground with scarcely room for their house and a garage.

"Was wondering if you'd have room for him out on the farm?" Uncle Bud continued. "Your boys would have fun with him. There's a harness and a cart, the whole works."

"I don't know, Bud. We got about all we can handle taking care of the cows, the pigs and the chickens. Don't think we'd have time to care for one more critter."

"Bob won't take no extra time. Fellow that I got him from just let him run loose. Said he didn't take no carin' for at all. You'd really be helping me out."

"Bring him," Pa finally said. I was glad he agreed. We didn't have a pony, bikes or anything like that. It'd be fun to be pulled around by a billy goat. Maybe we could even drive the goat over and show the Kolka boys. That'd sure knock their eyes out. Nobody that we knew had a goat of any kind. Here was one that could be harnessed and would pull a cart. We'd be the first in the neighborhood.

The next day Ross Caves, the local cattle trucker, drove into the yard. He stepped down from his red truck and walked over to the barn where he saw Pa and me working on the barnyard fence. He had a big smile on his face.

"Got a goat for you, Herm," Ross said.

The big white goat, with a white beard and two long curving horns, walked proudly down the truck ramp. "Baaaa," he said when he reached the ground—his way of saying hello, I imagined. A length of clothesline rope was wrapped around his neck. Ross handed me the end of the rope.

"Bob's his name," Ross said.

I pulled on the rope and Bob followed along behind me, just like a pony. I led him up to the house to show Ma while Ross and Pa unloaded the goat cart and harness.

"See my new goat," I said when I got to the back porch. Bob stepped right up on the porch and stood looking through the screen door into the kitchen.

Ma wasn't impressed. "Get that goat off the porch," she said. " 'Fore you know it that thing will be in the kitchen." Just then my twin brothers came running around the house. They surely liked what they saw as they ran up, and they began petting Bob.

Pa helped us harness and hitch Bob to the little goat cart that was just big enough to haul the twins, and he went back to working on the barnyard fence. My brothers climbed into the cart and I took the lead rope and said "giddap," just like I would to a horse. Bob just stood there and looked at me like I was speaking some foreign language. "Giddap," I said again. This time I pulled on the lead rope. But Bob didn't move.

> *Some of the best of what is next has been here all along.*

"Can't you get him to go?" my brother Don yelled.

"Don't know how to start him," I answered. "He don't seem to know horse talk."

"Give him a swat on the rump," Darrel said. I let go of the lead rope and walked around and gave Bob a slap on the behind. Well, that goat looked like he'd been shot out of a gun. He made one giant leap, which knocked off Don's straw hat, and went galloping down the driveway. My brothers were both yelling "whoa, whoa," but the goat keep on running—until he got to Ma's peony patch, where he stopped and began eating peony leaves.

"Some ride," Darrel said. He had yanked his straw hat down over his ears to keep it from flying off.

I dragged Bob away from the peonies and led him back near the barn. Pa stood there laughing. "Goat's got a few things to learn," he said.

We never did figure out how to make Bob pull the goat cart. He either didn't go at all or he charged off, scaring the bejeebers out of any kid riding in the cart.

He also had some bad habits. Ma put a little fence around her peonies, which kept Bob away, but then he turned to Ma's garden. Nobody messed with Ma's garden. One noon she told Pa she was gonna shoot that billy goat if she caught him in the garden again. We knew Ma wouldn't really do that because she'd never shot a gun in her life.

Pa was willing to put up with Bob's shenanigans when they involved Ma, but not long after the garden incident, Pa and Bob got personally involved with each other. I was sitting on the porch, whittling on a stick and watching the goat out the corner of one eye. Pa said I should keep an eye on the goat whenever I could so he didn't march back into Ma's garden. Pa was bending over, weeding the asparagus patch in front of the pump house. Bob was eating grass on the lawn,

> Some country roads are so crooked that you can see your taillights on the curves.

behaving himself as he had done all day. But what the goat saw was apparently too good to pass by.

Bob saw Pa all bent over with his rump up in the air. He put his head down so his horns were like two car bumpers and he galloped toward Pa, who didn't hear him coming.

Whomp. I heard the sound clear as a bell. Pa went head over teakettle, dang near hitting the barnyard fence. It was a comical thing to see. Pa got up, looked at Bob and commenced to cuss. I don't recall when I'd heard a richer set of swear words coming out of Pa. He called that billy goat about every name I'd ever heard and lots I hadn't.

The billy goat stood looking at Pa, shaking his head from time to time. I suspected Bob had been called names before. I knew that if Pa's shotgun had been handy, Bob would have been a goner.

Pa headed for the house. He walked right past me with not as much as an aye, yes or no, and rang up Uncle Bud.

"You can come get your dang goat," Pa said. He was still red in the face and breathing heavy.

The next day Ross Caves came for the goat and all its equipment.

"Goat didn't work out," Ross said, grinning.

"Nope," Pa answered. Pa wasn't grinning.

Milking Machine

Never trust a barn cat.

One day I heard Uncle Wilbur, who was a milk hauler, ask Pa, "When you getting a milkin' machine, Herm? Get your milkin' done a lot faster with a machine."

"Awful hard on the cows," Pa answered. "Way they tug and pull—can't believe they ain't painful."

"Cows get used to it," Uncle Wilbur answered. "Bunch of farmers got machines, you know."

That's the only time I ever heard Pa talk about milking machines. I figured we wouldn't get one—not with Pa feeling as he did. We had always milked cows by hand. "You get well acquainted with a cow when you milk by hand," Pa said. "And the cow gets to know you, too."

I considered several good reasons for buying a milking machine, besides getting the job done faster. A manure-drenched tail flaps in your face when you milk by hand, and a heavy cow foot comes down on your shoe from time to time and sends pain clear up to your eyeballs. But these are rather minor inconveniences compared to the antics of a mean cow. Just about the time you relax under such an animal and settle into a rhythm that sends milk squirting into the pail stuck between your legs, she kicks you over, spilling milk, bruising your leg or worse.

According to Pa, some annoyance is expected when hand milking. He often pointed out that every farm job had its good and bad features.

A few months after Uncle Wilbur mentioned "milking machine" Pa and I were in the Sears store in town, looking at the new Riteway models.

"We getting a milking machine?" I blurted out when we left the store.

"Yup," Pa said. "Gonna use some of the pig money." I knew Pa had just sold a truckload of hogs. Prices for pork were the best they'd been in years, with the war going on.

One afternoon the following week, when I got home from school, I saw that the milking machine had been installed. Pa was eager to demonstrate how it worked. He showed me the Briggs & Stratton engine and the vacuum pump. He held up one of the milking pails—it didn't look much different from a regular milk pail except it was bigger and had a cover with a rubber seal. Fastened to the cover were several long rubber tubes ending in four metal cup-like devices with rubber liners.

I couldn't wait to see the thing hanging on a cow and pulling milk out of her. After supper I saw it all firsthand. Pa gave a couple pulls on the engine's starter rope, and the machine began popping and the vacuum pump began pumping. The cows immediately began fidgeting and fussing from the noise.

Pa took a milker pail and set it between two cows. Then he stooped down with the teat cups in his hand. One after another he slid them into place on Mable's udder (Mable was the tamest of

> *No matter how fast things change, hold on to a few things that don't.*

our cows). With the milking machine, all four of Mable's teats could be milked at the same time. With hand milking, it was two at a time.

Mable looked around and cast a long glance at this strange shiny machine hanging on her udder, which was pulling and tugging. She shuffled her feet back and forth a couple times, then settled down to chewing her cud and enjoying this new experience.

"She likes it," I said.

"Guess so," Pa said, observing every movement of the cow and the machine.

Pa watched the milk spurt into the milk pail. When the spurts were few, he bent down, patted Mable on the side and removed the machine.

"Now you gotta strip her out," Pa instructed. "Finish milking her. Cream always comes last and we want to get all we can."

In the business of farming, it's not so important who gets there first as who gets there at all.

Pa worked right along, moving the machine from cow to cow while I milked out what the machine didn't. That is, until we came to Mildred. Mildred was the unpredictable one, the cow that would just as soon kick you on the leg as lick your hand.

The barn cats, as if anticipating trouble, had gathered in the aisle in back of Mildred, waiting. Four of them sat in a row—a black tom, a yellow female and a couple of half-grown kittens that were mottled in color.

Pa had no more than got the machine in place and stepped back to the aisle when Mildred let go with a hind foot. She caught the milking machine square on the top, tangling her foot in the rubber pipes. The first thrust of her massive hind leg lifted the entire milking machine pail off the floor, yanking the teat cups off her udder. The machine continued pulsing, sounding like a giant animal gasping for air. With each thrust of Mildred's rear leg, Pa tried to grab the bucket with its rubber tubes and flopping teat cups. Mildred continued trying to rid herself of this mechanical monster that had grabbed hold of her delicate teats. Kick as she might, she couldn't rid herself of this deep-breathing, metal and rubber creature that had tangled in her foot.

I started to laugh, but I immediately thought better of it and turned my head to muffle the sound. Pa and Mildred were doing a kind of dance, Pa dodging the cow's feet while trying to grab the bucket and Mildred shaking her hind foot like she'd stepped in a nest of hornets.

The machine eventually flew loose and rolled across the aisle in back of the cows, coming to a stop with a loud thud when it hit the wall. The barn cats scattered in four directions, with tails high and hair standing on end.

"Dang cow. Dang good-for-nothing cow," Pa was red in the face and furious. Mildred resumed chewing her cud, proud to have rid herself of a major annoyance.

"Mildred, you're a no-good cow. Do you hear me? Do you know what you just did, you dang cow?"

Mildred didn't even lift her head, didn't look around, didn't do anything but chew her cud.

I helped Pa gather up the pieces of his new milking machine, which was more dirtied up than damaged. We put the rubber pieces back together and Pa moved on to another cow.

Pa continued milking Mildred by hand until we sold her. She wanted nothing to do with the milking machine, no matter how gently Pa tried

> *One spring
> the winds were
> so strong
> everyone's land
> moved to the neighbors'.*

to introduce her to it.

Mildred was a good example of why modern laborsaving devices on the farm didn't always work as advertised. Cows, like people, have individual personalities. Some adapt to change easily, others don't.

Felix the Barn Cat

Don't climb trees.

Pa named the tomcat Felix. I don't know how he came up with such a name or why he named the cat at all. None of the other barn cats had names. At any one time we had a half-dozen cats that came by for a dish of milk each morning and evening when we were doing chores.

We didn't allow cats in the house, so some were on the wild order, never letting us pick them up or even get close to them. They were of multiple colors and sizes. Little brown ones, midsize yellow ones, full-grown multicolored ones. A rainbow of cat colors added a splash of contrast to the dreary barn with its faded walls that needed whitewashing.

The only time my brothers and I got close to the cats was when they were kittens. When a cat was expecting and she didn't show up for milk, we'd crawl into the hayloft and search for the kittens. Most of the time we'd find the nest, often when the little ones hadn't yet opened their eyes. We'd play with them, stroke them and hold them. We'd do this every day, until the kittens were big enough to come down to the milk bowl.

We'd found Felix and his littermates shortly

after they were born. Felix, completely black except for a pink nose and a white-tipped tail, was the largest cat in his litter. He grew up to be a big tom, one of the biggest cats we'd ever had in the barn.

Different from other tomcats we'd known—toms were always courting our females—Felix was friendly and mild-mannered. Some of the visiting toms were outlaws. They'd bite you on the leg or scratch your hand if you stooped down to pet them. The bowl of fresh milk every day attracted them to the barn. One visiting tom caught my attention because he obviously was a fighter, although apparently not a very good one. He was a skinny yellow cat that always looked liked he'd just rolled in the dirt. He carried many battle scars—the tip of his tail was missing, one ear hung limp and his left eye was permanently closed. When you got close to

> *Best thing to do when you find yourself in a hole is to quit digging.*

him, he hunched his back, glared at you with his good eye and growled.

Felix, on the other hand, liked to have his back rubbed and enjoyed people. He'd brush up against Pa's pant leg and begin purring loudly as soon as Pa started doing chores. Another thing that set Felix apart was his walk. No sulking around the corners and sneaking up to the milk dish. Felix walked proudly down the center of the aisle in back of the cows with his head up and his tail high. Maybe it was his size, or perhaps just his demeanor, but the other cats stepped aside when Felix approached. The wild ones and even the yellow fighter with the torn ear and the blind eye avoided Felix. No doubt about it, Felix was the boss cat in our barn.

When Pa bought the milking machine, the atmosphere in the barn changed. Before it had been exceedingly quiet, except for the sounds of cattle rustling their hay, horses munching grain and calves jumping around in the calf pen. Now there were new sounds. During milking, the barn was filled with the "pop-pop" of the Briggs & Stratton engine running the vacuum pump and the wheezing of the milking machine units.

For several days after the milking machine was installed, none of the cats appeared at the milk bowl. Then slowly they returned, first Felix, then the other semi-tame cats and finally the wild ones that were most skittish about the new sounds in the barn.

Felix was a curious cat. I doubt there was a corner of the barn, or the other farm buildings for that matter, that he didn't know intimately. He took it upon himself to get acquainted with the noisy milking machine. The gasoline engine that ran the vacuum pump with a V belt was located on a little platform just as you came in the barn door. The belt ran over two pulleys—a small one on the gasoline engine, and a larger one on the vacuum pump.

I saw Felix standing beneath the engine and vacuum pump, looking up, his long tail swinging back and forth. Not long after, I saw him on the platform—there was just enough room for the big cat and the milking machine equipment. Soon this became his resting place while we milked. On cold winter days, the engine and vacuum pump threw off enough heat to make this a cozy spot.

Pa anticipated what was about to happen before my brothers and I did. One day he said, "That milking machine belt is gonna catch old Felix's tail." It wasn't more than a day later that it happened, just like Pa said it would. I was working in the middle of the barn when I heard the most terrifying scream. I looked at the platform and there was Felix, all four legs extended straight, his neck outstretched, sailing around

> *There is less mud on the top of the hill.*

and around as if something had him by the tail, which was the case. He had stuck his tail where no cat tail should ever go. By the time Pa got to the machine to shut it down, Felix had been flung against the wall. He now stood on the floor, dazed. He shook his head a couple times and, obviously confused, tore off at top speed under the cows, covering the entire length of the barn with a few mighty leaps. The cows jumped as he ran under them, tearing at their stanchions and kicking frantically. Pandemonium had taken over the barn. Upon reaching the end of the barn, Felix turned and headed down the aisle in back of the cows, yowling with each leap. Pa yelled, "Open the door," which I did. Felix shot through the opening, covered the several hundred yards to the woods in back of the house in seconds and disappeared into the underbrush.

> *The homeliest cow in the barn usually gives the most milk.*

"Probably won't see old Felix again," Pa said.

"Too bad, he was a good cat," I said.

"He was that. Little too nosy for his own good, though."

"I guess so," I replied.

A week later, Felix returned triumphantly. He paraded down the barn aisle with his head held high and his tail raised. But now, rather than sticking out straight behind him, Felix's tail had a right angle to it, about a third of the way from the end. As he walked south, his tail pointed west.

"There's old Felix," I announced when I first saw him.

"Got a little problem with his tail," Pa said.

"Got a big problem," I said, laughing.

But Felix never let his right-pointing tail interfere with his life on the farm or his control over the cats in the barn. The other barn cats didn't seem to care which way Felix's tail pointed. One thing was different, though. He never again rested on the platform near the milking machine. In fact, when he walked past the equipment, he growled deep down in his throat to let the mechanical monster know that it may have won a little skirmish, but that he, Felix, still ruled the barn and all that was in it.

Fireworks

You can't teach an old horse new tricks.
Good thing: who wants an old horse doing tricks?

It was a long-standing Fourth of July tradition. Families gathered for a chicken dinner served by the volunteer firefighters at the church hall in the village. Farmers sat around in the shade, discussing the weather, farm prices, politics, and what was happening to the country. A long line of people waited to pay for their meal and have a firefighter put half a barbecued chicken on a paper plate, followed by a mound of mashed potatoes with gravy, a scoop of coleslaw, a dill pickle and a slab of apple pie. You got your own coffee from a big shiny urn at the end of the table.

I knew that something about this Fourth of July would be different when the fire whistle blew and the volunteer firefighters disappeared, abandoning the ticket sales counter and all the serving stations. People standing in line just stood dumbstruck for a few minutes. Then someone from the crowd sat down and began selling tickets, someone else started handing out barbecued chicken and the serving continued. The volunteer firefighters didn't return and people wondered what had happened. (Later we learned they had responded to a serious car accident.)

As the sun began slipping away and dusk crept over the village, everyone gathered around the millpond, on the east side and on the south side, and especially on the north side where they could stand on the bridge that spanned the river and watch the fireworks. This year's fireworks display, according to the promotion in the paper, included a new, more powerful aerial bomb never before seen in this part of the country. It was truly something that everyone looked forward to.

The crowd thickened as darkness slowly crept across the millpond, silhouetting the homes along the shore and the ice shanties that had been pulled up on the bank before the ice went out in the spring. Little wisps of steam began rising from the warm millpond water as the air cooled. Crowd talk was subdued, a low murmur that drifted across the stillness of the millpond's surface.

Save string.

Kaboom! The first aerial bomb shot out of its tube, rushed into the cloudless sky and exploded with a thunderous roar. The crowd cheered. Only a few more minutes and the fireworks would begin.

The streetlights popped on. Not enough light to spoil the aerial show but enough to find your way back to your car when it was finished.

The crowd was becoming impatient. There were bursts of clapping, especially on the bridge, which was closest to the village taverns. Then more clapping and another aerial bomb. Kaboom. The clapping stopped, briefly, then began once more. It was time. The officials in charge had waited as long as possible. Start too early and they were criticized, "Colors weren't good, sky too bright." Wait too long and, "Cripes, we're keeping the kids up half the night."

"Whoosh" and then "pop" and the sky filled with a circle of color—reds and blues, oranges and yellows. Hanging just briefly, just long enough to enjoy and then sputtering out and dropping into the millpond with a soft sizzle.

Clapping and cheering. Each display a little more spectacular than the last. Babies crying. Little children holding their ears. Young lovers not watching, creating their own fireworks, their own sizzle.

But where was the big one? The advertised super aerial bomb. The granddaddy of all fireworks. Or had we already heard it and not noticed?

Had it been one of the earlier bombs, the ones that were truly loud and attention-getting but not noisier than most people had heard before?

Now a brief pause. Was the show finished? No finale? I along with many others surmised they were preparing the big bomb for lighting. Across the pond to the west we could see men working, carrying the little lighted torches they used to ignite the various aerial displays.

We saw them touch a torch to a long tube. Ordinarily they just turned their backs when they lit a tube, but this time they turned and ran. This surely must be the one. This must be the advertised giant aerial bomb.

But rather than blasting into the sky, we saw a sparking, smoking missile skidding along the shore of the millpond. The tall tube had tipped over. In an instant the giant bomb had crashed into one of the fish shanties on shore and then exploded. Pieces of fish shanty flew halfway across the pond.

The sound of the explosion shook the ground. People stood aghast, their mouths hanging open. Those most frightened turned to run but there was no place to go—too many people.

And then it was quiet. Deathly quiet. A few pieces of smoking fish shanty floated on the surface of the millpond. Somebody on the bridge let out a loud cheer. And then everyone clapped, a loud thunderous applause. More cheering. Clearly this had been the best of all aerial bombs, even though it was the fish shanty that lifted into the air and not the bomb.

Then, the fireworks crew set off the finale, a cluster of displays—Uncle Sam, the American flag, a waterfall, multiple aerial bursts—which lighted the sky from horizon to horizon, and succeeded in shutting off all the streetlights that were on light sensors. People stumbled in the dark toward their cars. It was a Fourth of July to remember.

Uncle Fred and the Ducks

When it's too late to do something, it's usually too late.

The fog was so thick that Pa and I could scarcely see from the barn to the pump house. We'd finished milking and were on our way to the house and breakfast. The old elm tree by the back porch was dripping moisture. Fanny, our cow dog, stayed on the porch, out of the wet.

In the kitchen, Ma was busy at the woodstove frying pancakes for breakfast. "Flapjacks'll go good on a morning like this," she said. She worked over a cast iron griddle that fried eight pancakes at a time. As fast as she made a batch, they disappeared as my twin brothers, Pa and I sat at the table, slicing up brown cakes and downing them. Earlier, Ma'd fried up a bunch of thick bacon slices and we smeared bacon grease on our pancakes before drenching them in dark brown Karo syrup.

"Morning like this reminds me of a fall day when I was a kid," Pa said. When Pa started out like this, it usually meant a story. Pa had grown up on a sandy, hilly farm about three miles from our place, in an area sprinkled with lakes and known as Skunk's Hollow to the inhabitants. Pa liked to tell stories about his growing-up years on that old farm. Many of his stories centered on the lakes. The tales ranged from trapping skunks and making skunk grease to fishing bullheads and catching snapping turtles and making soup out of them.

"I remember it was foggy, worse than today. My brother Fred and I decided that there just might be some ducks on the pond. Flock goin' south may have lit there to wait for the weather to clear."

Pa lifted his coffee cup, took a drink, and then continued.

"There was this woods you had to go through before you got to the pond so Fred and I headed off. Fred carried his double-barrel ten-gauge shotgun. It was a beast of a gun, heavy as carryin' a lead pipe. And kick? Why, that thing sent your shoulder into spasms, like an old plow horse had let loose with a hind leg and hit you square in the shoulder."

"Any more takers on flapjacks?" Ma asked.

"I'll have a couple more," I replied. Nothing tasted better than flapjacks and bacon grease on a dreary, soggy morning like this one.

"So here we are, sneakin' through the woods toward the pond, Fred and me," Pa continued. "Trees was drippin' a little moisture but not so much as to be a bother. Foggier than a bugger, though. Could hardly see the end of Fred's gun barrel."

I was eating pancakes and listening; so were the twins. We didn't want to miss a word of what was coming because this was a story we hadn't heard before.

"Well, Fred and me, we hunkered down and eased through the woods toward that pond, trying not to make a sound, trying not to snap any twigs or break off any low-hangin' branches. We still didn't know if we'd find any ducks there. But as we got closer we picked up a sound like a flock of chickens workin' in a barnyard."

"Was it chickens you heard?" I asked.

"It wasn't chickens, just sounded that way. It was ducks. Wild ducks. And it sounded like a lot of 'em. A big flock. I whispered to Fred, 'There's ducks out there on that pond, a lot of 'em.'

"Fred, he just nods and motions for me to be quiet. I stopped in my tracks, forcing my ears to hear through the fog."

Pa stopped talking for an instant and lifted up his coffee cup. "You got any more coffee in that pot, Ma?"

Ma came over and poured Pa's cup full. My brothers and I just sat there, waiting for him to go on with the story.

"Well, Fred and me, we sneaked on through the brush, quiet as can be. We still couldn't see the pond, it was so dang foggy. But the duck sounds got louder so we knew we was close.

"Before you could say holy cow, there was the pond right in front of us. I almost stepped in it."

"What about the ducks?" my brother Don blurted out.

"They was there all right. In the mist were all those ducks. Mallards, I think they were. Big ducks, cackling away like so many chickens. A bunch of shadows floatin' on the water. Almost invisible out there in the fog.

"Something must have scared 'em or one of those ducks that keeps watch must have seen us, because the whole dang flock just took off at once, quacking away like I'd never heard. More noise than I ever knowed ducks to make. I suspect the fog made it sound louder.

"I yelled to Fred, 'Shoot! Shoot!' He pulls back both hammers on the double-barrel and yanks back both triggers at once. Kaboom. The sound of the ten-gauge just about knocked me over. But it was nothin' like the pain Fred was feelin' after the stock of that old shotgun slammed into his shoulder."

"Did Fred kill any ducks?" I asked.

"Kill any ducks? Kill any ducks?" Pa said. "Why, there was ducks fallin' out of the sky all around us. It was rainin' down ducks. They were droppin' out of the fog one after the other. We gathered up eight. There's few hunters that get that many ducks with one shot. But Fred did. And it's the truth, too."

Pa leaned back in his chair and took another sip of coffee. I looked at the twins and we all began laughing. Pa just smiled. Ma said quietly, "Sounds like you stretched that one a little, Herm."

Floyd's Woods

*If you are mad at your neighbor and are compelled to tell him off,
practice your speech on your farm dog. With the words off your chest,
you'll feel better, and your dog will appreciate the attention he's gotten.*

It was the night before the opening of deer season and the neighborhood boys had gathered around our kitchen table to plan strategy, tell stories of past hunts and sip a little homemade wine. But mostly it was a serious discussion because deer hunting had become a highly competitive activity. Not only was it a major shortcoming to not bag a buck, but shooting one with less than six points was clearly a limited success. Worst of all was when a buck could have been bagged—or so everyone agreed—and the hunter had a tinge of buck fever and missed. That moment of failure was never forgotten, even if it had occurred ten years in the past. It came up at every kitchen table gathering without fail, year after year. "Remember, Jim, when that ten-pointer stood right in front of you and we were all watching, and you aimed and aimed, finally fired, and the deer bounded off without a scratch?"

But this year, a nagging topic took center place. Everyone agreed that the big bucks, the ten-pointers and larger, somehow knew to gather in Floyd Jeffer's woods. Floyd didn't allow hunting, didn't even allow you to walk on his land. Some thought Floyd was saving his big woods for himself. But that wasn't so because Floyd didn't hunt. He didn't hunt squirrels or rabbits. Didn't hunt pheasants or ruffed grouse. He didn't hunt anything. In a community where everyone hunted, here was a holdout, a non-hunter in a hunting community.

Floyd was a bachelor who lived alone on a poor sandy farm, much of it wooded, where he milked a few bony Guernsey cows, put up a few loads of hay, and harvested a small crib of corn each year. He walked bent over, supported by a crooked homemade walking stick.

Floyd had nailed big metal "No Trespassing" signs on trees and fence posts every few yards all the way around his farm. This was during a time, in the late 1940s and 1950s, when farmers didn't post their land but allowed their neighbors to roam freely across the countryside. Farmers in the community had miles of hunting territory, including wooded lands, marshes and acres of corn and hay fields. The only interruption in this vast hunting territory was Floyd's farm, a one-hundred-sixty-acre island in the midst of several thousand acres of open hunting land.

> *Fellow went to his country school reunion. Met a classmate he hadn't seen in years. He said she had aged so much she didn't even recognize him.*

"I just know it," my brother Don offered as discussion moved around to Floyd's property. "I just know that's where them big ones are holed up. They're smart, them big deer. They know where to go and it's in Floyd's woods."

"Yup," Jim Kolka agreed. "You're right. We ought get into them woods and roust the big ones out of there."

I stayed quiet during the discussion. I knew Floyd Jeffers and I knew what he thought about hunters and hunting.

"How we gonna do it?" Don asked, pushing the subject one more time. There was silence around the table as the hunters sipped a little more of Pa's homemade, god-awful grape wine. They sipped to be polite if nothing more.

Eyes turned in my direction. "Jerry, you know Floyd better than any of us, right?"

"Maybe," I said, because I knew where the conversation was headed.

"How'd it be if you sneak into his woods tomorrow and kick those big bucks outta there? If he catches you, won't be no problem cause he knows who you are."

"Not that simple," I said without elaborating. I knew Floyd's strong feelings about hunting, especially deer hunting.

"You gotta do it, Jerry," Jim Kolka said. "It's your duty, you owe it to the rest of us."

I couldn't see how I owed this group the opportunity to be chewed out by Floyd when he caught me trespassing in his woods, but I finally agreed to do it, with the hope I could

> *Don't listen in on party-line telephone calls, but when you do, avoid sharing the gossip.*

chase out the big ones and not be spotted.

Floyd had lean, craggy features. His face was wrinkled like an old piece of harness leather and his eyes were deep-set in a pair of hollows. It was his eyes that people noticed. He had intense gray eyes that bored right through you.

On opening day of deer season, Jim Kolka dropped me off on the far side of Floyd's woods and the boys gathered at Coombes' place where they knew the big ones would run. I hadn't been in Floyd's big woods fifteen minutes when I heard a twig snap behind me. I wheeled around, expecting to see a squirrel or maybe a big buck. But there stood Floyd in his faded blue barn coat. He had appeared from nowhere.

"Jerry, you know you're not supposed to hunt here."

> *If you must brag,*
> *do it humbly.*

"I know that, Floyd," I answered, feeling guilty that I'd agreed to test his resolve. I didn't argue with him, didn't try to tell him I was lost and had strayed onto his property by mistake. He would know I was lying the minute I opened my mouth. I turned around and walked to the road as fast as I could. I could feel Floyd's piercing gray eyes boring into my back, following me out of his woods, keeping me honest as was sometimes necessary with young men who pushed limits and tested authority.

"How come you're outta there so fast?" Jim Kolka inquired when he saw me.

"Floyd kicked me out," I said. "Knew he would."

"Thought you knew him," Jim said.

"Didn't matter, he still kicked me out."

And so the hunting season passed and no

one bagged a big buck. Same thing the next year and the year after. Except now we all had an excuse.

"Big ones are in Floyd's woods," we agreed.

I doubted they were, but it was a useful excuse. When you are less than successful it helps to have a reason for your ineptness that no one will challenge.

Sandburs and Watermelons

The reason farmers complain even when things are going well is they know the good times never last, and they want to stay in practice.

The wind whistled around the corner of the house and snow began piling up on the back porch. Ma popped a pan of popcorn on the kitchen stove and we all gathered around, eating popcorn and listening to the storm.

"Did I ever tell you about the time we swiped some of Billy Carpenter's watermelons?" Pa began.

Even if we'd heard the story, we knew we were going to hear it again. When Pa got started on a tale, he didn't stop just because somebody said they'd heard it before. Besides, a story never came out quite the same way twice; there were always some twists and turns and new events added.

"Well, it was a cool night in late September. Full moon, as I recall. No wind. Just as clear as a bell. Been better if it was cloudy. Been better for Sid and me."

"Sid Simon?" Ma asked. Sid was a farmer about Pa's age, but a little shorter than Pa.

"Yup. I saw Sid in the village that afternoon and Sid said that he'd just heard about Billy Carpenter's big melon patch off Highway 73.

" 'Biggest melons in this part of the county and they ought to be ripe by now,' Sid said.

"I knew about Billy Carpenter and I tell Sid that I'm not sure we wanna try swiping his melons.

" 'Why's that?' Sid asks.

"I tell him that I heard Billy sits out by his melon patch with a double-barrel shotgun each night, protecting his melons from guys like us. Sid, he just laughs and says he's not concerned about any shotgun, not when the melons are ripe.

"Well, that night Sid comes by with his Model T Ford, picks me up and we head toward Billy Carpenter's place. We park the car in the Willow Grove school-yard on Highway 73 and walk down the road toward Billy's farm. It's about a half-mile or so.

"I remember the moon being about as bright as it ever gets. It was near as bright as a cloudy day at noon. You could see just about everything. We headed across a cow pasture and then we came up on a little rise. There they were. Watermelons. Big melons everywhere. About the most melons I'd ever seen in one field.

"Well, we no more than picked off the first couple of melons and shoved them into the

When people asked Sam how he was, he always replied, "I'm no better than I aughta be."

gunny bags we was carryin', when we hears a 'kaboom.' It was so dang loud it knocked me over, as it did Sid. We each thought the other was shot.

"We looked off toward Billy's place and there he was, standing on the hill on the far end of the patch with his shotgun.

" 'Git outta my melon patch or you're goners!' Billy yelled. We both agreed about the same time that we'd better hustle on outta there.

"Sid whispered that we ought to crawl in a direction different from the one we came, in case Billy had been watchin' right from the beginning. We had far less chance gettin' shot when we was crawlin'. We was soon in an old grain field, and it was full of sandburs, the kind that dig into your hide and hang on.

"We'd just started crawlin' when Billy shot again. This time we saw the fire fly out the end of his shotgun. We hadn't gotten ten yards and there was another blast. I'll bet we set some kind of record for crawlin', to say nothing about the amount of sandburs that we'd accumulated.

"Finally we gets back to the car. We spent the next hour pulling sandburs out of each other. I noticed that Sid's overalls were wet in front. I didn't ask if he'd had an accident out there in the melon patch, but I knew he had.

"We never did go back to Billy Carpenter's place. Blame sandburs were worse than his shotgun."

Pa often had a moral to his stories, especially when they involved mischief such as trying to swipe watermelons.

"Let this be a lesson to you, boys," he said. "Try to do something wrong, and you get punished one way or the other."

"Yes, Pa," we said in unison.

What I'd learned from the story is don't try to swipe watermelons when the moon is full and there are a lot of sandburs around.

ENTRY
TAG

1604

EXHIBITOR   Junior/4-H
                   40-185-18503

Department: 4
Class: 0
Lot: 10

Plant & Soil

ENTRY
TAG

EXHIBITOR

Department:
Class:
Lo

Plant & Soi
Vegetable G
Carrots, 4

1707

Junior/4-H
-185-1850

Expensive Lesson

Appreciate cool water from your well on a hot summer day.

"You can learn a lot at a county fair," Pa always said. I remember one year, when I was maybe six or seven years old, Pa and I were strolling down the midway past the games and booths, watching men take aim at the shooting gallery, seeing people toss darts at multicolored balloons ("win a panda bear"), when we stopped in front of a tent with an immense banner strung between two red posts. On the banner, in printing that could be seen halfway across the fairgrounds, were the words: SEE THE HORSE WITH ITS TAIL WHERE ITS HEAD OUGHT TO BE.

"Will you look at that?" Pa said. "Got to be some strange kind of horse." People were lined up in front of a ticket booth where a grizzled old man with wrinkled brown skin and watery eyes sat selling tickets.

"Got a picture of that horse?" Pa asked the old man, who wore a little flat-topped white straw hat.

"Nope, ain't got a picture. Go in and have a look, only one thin quarter."

"Whatta you think, Jerry? Worth fifty cents for us to see this horse with its tail where its head ought to be?"

I agreed that it was probably worth the money. Pa plunked down fifty cents and we followed the line of people into the dark, hot tent that smelled like timothy hay, horse manure and sawdust.

For a brief time we didn't see anything, and then, when our eyes adjusted to the darkness, we saw this most unusual of all horses. People inside the tent just stood there staring, not saying anything. All were as surprised as we were. Then Pa said under his breath, "We been snookered."

There was a horse there all right, a big, brown Belgian with a cream-colored mane. But there wasn't one thing unusual about that big brown horse, except he had been backed into his stall so his rear end was up against his manger. The sign was right, the horse had his tail where his head ought to be.

Pa was so mad he'd have clobbered the horse's owner, but there was nobody around, except for the wrinkled old gray-haired man selling tickets. The old man smiled at Pa when we came out of the tent. Pa started to open his mouth. I knew he wanted to tell the long line of people waiting to pay their money that the horse was a fraud. But he didn't. Later I asked him why. "Quarter ain't too much to waste on a lesson folks will never forget," he said.

Restaurant Meal

Having a fancy house and a shabby barn
is like having an expensive car but not being able to afford gasoline.

I could scarcely sleep the night before, thinking about the coming trip to Milwaukee. The morning we were to leave, Ma made sure I wore clean underwear, newly washed overalls and my school shirt. She even made me comb my hair before I put on my cap.

Promptly at eight, the big red cattle truck pulled into our yard. Pa and Ross Caves, the truck's owner, loaded a couple of calves and Ross said, "Well, Jerry, you ready?"

"I am," I answered as I stepped up to the running board and then into the truck. I had never been inside something this big before. Ross Caves often asked a neighbor kid to ride with him to the stockyards in Milwaukee and now it was my turn. I made myself comfortable on the well-worn seat and waited while Ross and Pa talked some before Ross crawled in and slammed the door.

The engine roared to life and soon we were headed down the driveway. I waved to Ma and Pa who were standing on the porch. "Gotta stop at Kolka's and pick up a cow, then we'll be on our way," Ross said.

The truck rumbled along the dusty road past the back side of our farm. I noticed it rode a lot rougher than our car and made a lot more noise. Soon we were pulling into Kolka's yard. Ross backed the truck up to the barn and I rolled down my window to talk with the Kolka boys.

"I'm going to the stockyards in Milwaukee," I said, "and I'll be eating in a restaurant at noon." No farm kid ever ate in a restaurant, and I could see the Kolka boys were envious of my good fortune. I suppose I could have said that Ross would likely ask them to go along on a future trip, but I didn't mention that possibility. I didn't want to do anything to tarnish the fact that today was my special trip.

Slowly we drove down Kolka's hill and then turned onto County Highway A and speeded up some. I felt the truck rock as the animals in the back shifted when we turned the corner.

"Animals will settle down once we travel a few miles," Ross said. And they did. I sat back in my seat, looking out the window at the red barns and silos, at the cows in pasture. It was June and the countryside was every shade of green.

We drove through a small town every few miles. Ross slowed down and I looked at the buildings, at the grocery stores, at the five-and-dime stores, at the brick banks and barbershops with striped poles out front. I noticed the little restaurants with the words "Eat" or "Home Cooking" prominently displayed in their windows. I wondered if the restaurant where we'd eat would be like one of these. Occasionally I saw kids on the street that looked my age. I waved at them, wanting them to see that I had a chance to ride in a cattle truck all the way to Milwaukee. Sometimes they waved back, but often they merely turned away, not responding.

Just before noon we began approaching Milwaukee with its tall buildings and new smells.

> *Lots of folks work hard at doing nothing.*

Ross said some of the strange smells came from the breweries—he mentioned Blatz, Schlitz, Pabst and Miller. Soon we drove into the Milwaukee stockyards and confronted a new set of sounds, smells and sights. I could see livestock pens, hundreds of them. Narrow aisles separated the pens from each other. I saw two men on horseback, wearing cowboy hats and carrying lariats in their hands, herding cattle from one pen to another with considerable yelling and cussing. Smells of livestock manure, truck exhaust, dry hay and human sweat all tangled together, creating a rather unpleasant aroma that no one mentioned.

When Ross finished unloading his truck, he asked, "You hungry?"

"Sure," I said.

"About time for lunch."

I thought it a little strange he said "lunch."

> *George Dietrich said he was fed up with politics. Said he was switching his alienation from the Republicans to the Democrats.*

Lunch usually amounted to only a cookie or so, nothing that would fill you up. I was hoping we'd have dinner.

I followed Ross into the Stockyards Restaurant, located not far from the unloading docks. Once inside the busy place, the smells quickly changed to those of onions frying, coffee brewing and hamburgers grilling.

This was the first time I had ever been inside a restaurant. I watched what Ross did to make sure I didn't do something dumb. Ross pulled out a chair by the window and sat down. I sat down opposite him. So far so good. The table was bare except for a pair of salt and pepper shakers, a bottle of Heinz ketchup (that's what it said on the label; we always called it cat soup), and what I figured must be a sugar bowl. I looked around, and there were men sitting at nearly all the tables, some of them smoking pipes, several with cigarettes hanging out of their mouths, but most of them just eating. Of course everybody was talking at once and I couldn't make hide nor hair out of what they were saying.

I'd no more than gotten one good look around when a young woman wearing a neat little flowered apron came to our table. She plunked down a glass of water in front of each of us. Then she handed Ross and me each a good-sized piece of cardboard. On this cardboard was printed a list of about every food you could imagine. I ran my eye down the line-up: Swiss steak, fried ham, T-bone steak, hamburger steak, meatballs and gravy, pork chops, sauerkraut and pork hocks, sauerkraut and sausage, fried chicken. I'd never seen anything like it, never imagined somebody could find so many different kinds of food in one place. Everything had a price behind it, too.

Fellow in the village said he could run so fast that he got to where he was going before he left.

"Our special today is roast beef with mashed potatoes and peas," the young woman said. "Fifty cents."

Ross didn't even look at the cardboard before he handed it back to the young woman.

"I'll take the special," he said. "What do you want, Jerry? Treats on me." I wanted to tell Ross that Ma had given me a dollar so I could buy both our lunches. But there didn't seem time here to explain all this with the young woman waiting.

"You want a minute to look at the menu?" she asked as she pointed to the cardboard. I'd flipped it over and was looking at the list of pies—apple, cherry, lemon, chocolate, mincemeat, pecan (I wondered what that was) and several more.

"I'll take the special, too," I blurted out, handing the cardboard back to the young woman. She smiled.

"And what will you be having to drink?" she inquired.

"Coffee for me. What about you, Jerry?"

"Do you have milk?"

"Sure."

"Then that's what I'll have."

Soon the young woman was back with our silverware wrapped with big paper napkins. I was surprised to see the napkins. The only time Ma brought out the napkins was at Christmas and Thanksgiving and when our city relatives visited. The rest of the time if you got something on your hands you wiped them off on your pants.

Ross unwrapped his knife, fork and spoon and I did, too.

Before I could look around another time, she was back with our meals. The smell was wonderful. The meat was thick and juicy and even the mashed potatoes were good. I didn't think anybody could fix mashed potatoes better than Ma,

> *Some bridges should be crossed before you get to them.*

but these came close. The peas were a disappointment. They were limp and mushy. I wanted to say something about that but thought better of it. I suspected city people ran this restaurant, and they didn't have much chance to sink their teeth into peas fresh from the garden. The biggest disappointment of all was the bread—a couple of limp slices of white bakery bread. At home we always had homemade bread, thickly sliced. Pa said it was best to eat homemade bread because it stuck to your ribs. I sunk my teeth into this bakery bread and kept my mouth shut about what Pa said.

The milk surprised me most. I had never tasted milk like it, and I drank milk every day. The milk here was cold and it was wonderful. Our icebox at home never cooled milk down like what I had in my glass.

Soon my plate was clean and Ross asked if I wanted any dessert. He said he was having apple pie with a dip of ice cream. I said that would be fine with me and soon I was digging into the best-tasting piece of apple pie I'd ever stuck in my mouth. The ice cream made it even better.

Once more the young woman came by but this time with a slip of paper she handed to Ross. Ross said it was the bill, and he looked at it carefully. I said Ma had given me some money for lunch.

"I'll pay," Ross said. "But you can leave the tip."

"What's a tip?" I asked.

"Oh, you leave a little money on the table for the waitress. Fifteen cents should be about right."

I fished in my pocket for a dime and a nickel and put them on the table, and I stood behind Ross while he stopped at the cash register to pay. I couldn't wait to get home and tell Ma and Pa about what I had to eat. I especially wanted to tell the Kolka boys about eating in a restaurant. I wanted to tell them about the

cardboard with the long list of foods, about how milk tasted when it was cold and that you always left a little extra money on the table for the girl who brought you the food. I decided I wouldn't mention the soggy peas and the limp bakery bread.

Soon we were back in the truck and on our way home. I doubt we were even out of Milwaukee when I fell asleep. I didn't wake up until we were more than halfway home. Ross was humming a little tune as we bounced along the highway, going a bit faster with an empty truck.

When he approached our farm, I thanked him and said he could just drop me off at the bottom of our driveway. I ran up the hill and burst into the house. Ma was setting plates around the table, preparing for supper. I couldn't wait to tell her how they did things in a restaurant and how they used napkins every day, not only on Christmas, Thanksgiving

> *When you go out on a limb, make sure no one with a saw is in sight.*

and when city relatives came. I also told her how confused city people were. Ross and I sat down and ate dinner, and they called it lunch. I told Ma how I'd asked Ross about this and he said that city people eat dinner in the evening. I guessed they didn't know about supper. I told Ma, "At times like this, I'm sure glad I live in the country—although I did have a good time in Milwaukee, especially at the restaurant."

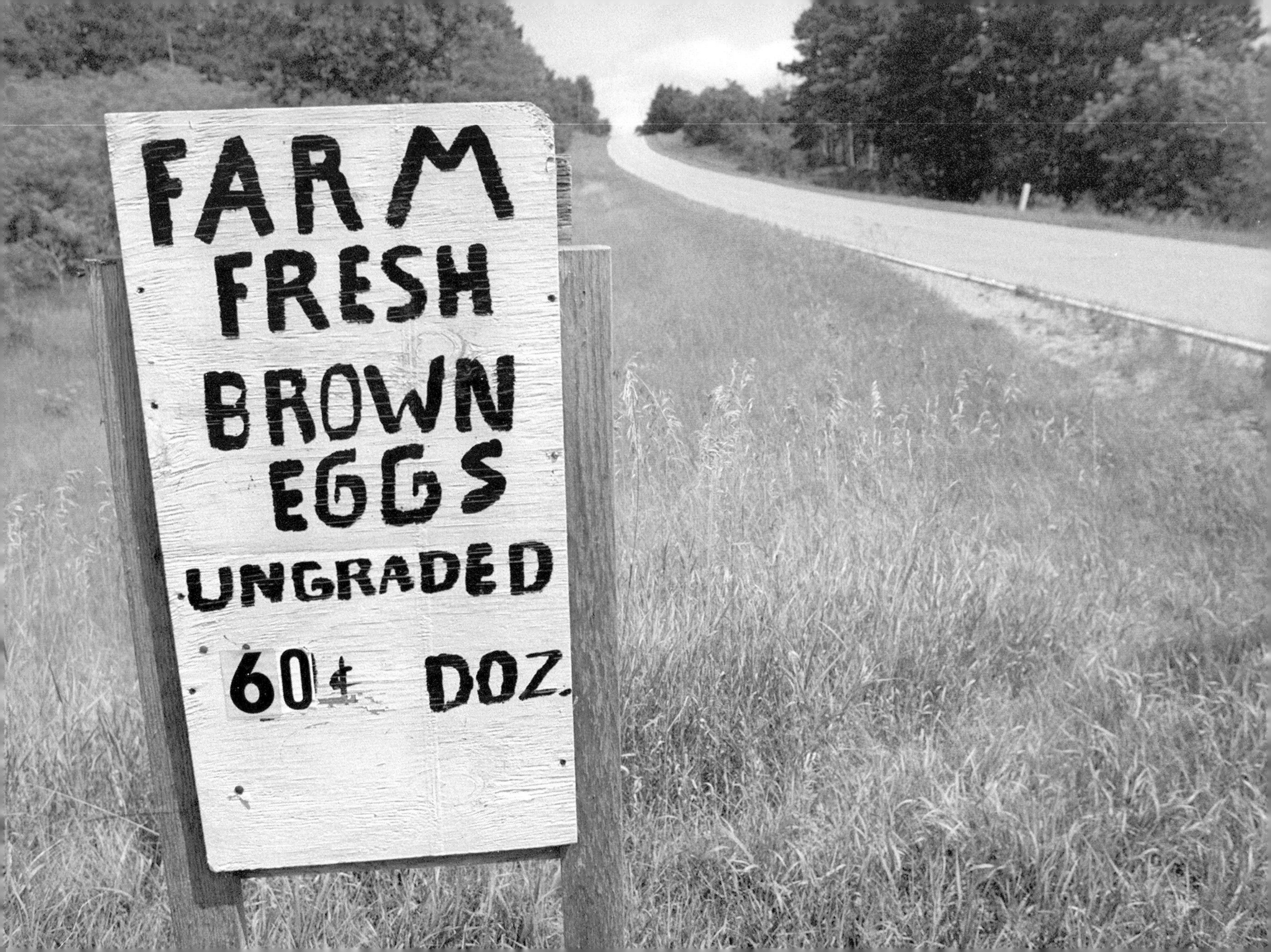
FARM
FRESH
BROWN
EGGS
UNGRADED
60¢ DOZ.

Dietrich's Laying Hens

Farmer in the eastern part of the state just won the lottery.
He says he's now able to farm a few more years.

Folks never knew what to expect from our new neighbor, George Dietrich, who had moved to the Chain O' Lake community from the city with his wife and two boys. Without half trying, he had challenged long-standing ways of doing things and even basic rural truths. For instance, one day he stopped at our farm, as he often did, with an important announcement. That's what he called it anyway. Nobody in our community would ever say "important announcement." Yet, here was George, standing on our back porch with a big smile on his face while Pa stood listen-ing. Pa had heard a slug of George's important messages over the past several months, but was trying to be neighborly and polite.

"It's my laying hens," George said.

"Something wrong with 'em?"

"Just the opposite."

"Whatta you mean?"

"They're laying more eggs than they are sup-posed to."

"How so?" Pa said, a look of disbelief spread-ing across his face.

"Well, I got twenty hens, bought them from a

fellow on the other side of the county."

"You told me that before."

"On Tuesday I got seventeen eggs."

"That's pretty good," Pa said.

"Wednesday I got nineteen."

"Nineteen," Pa repeated, not believing what he'd heard.

"Thursday I got twenty-one."

"Impossible," Pa blurted out. "Can't get more eggs than you got chickens. A hen can't lay more than one egg a day."

"Well, mine can, Herman. Because yesterday I got twenty-five eggs."

"You don't say," Pa said, now smiling. He thought George had probably spent too much time around Norman Mueller, who was well known for his ability to stretch the truth.

"It's the truth and I want you to come over and look at my hens. They are clearly something special."

"They sure must be," Pa said. "I'll stop over

April on the farm builds character and challenges optimism.

tomorrow."

Pa and I drove over to Dietrich's place the next day. George had already invited Frank Kolka, who lived across the road. Frank was looking at Dietrich's flock of laying hens digging around in the chicken yard. I looked them over and didn't see anything special. They looked like an ordinary flock of white leghorns.

"Layin' more than one egg a day?" Pa said.

"That's correct," George answered.

Frank Kolka was scratching his head, not believing what he was hearing. After a while Frank said, "See that hen over there?" He pointed to a white chicken that looked a little different from the others. "That's my hen, and so is that one on the far side of the yard."

"Can't be," George said. "Can't be."

"Chicken only has to walk across the road to get here," Frank said.

"George, Frank's chickens are laying eggs in your chicken house. Nothing special about your

chickens, except for their ability to invite the neighbor's hens over to lay eggs in your henhouse." Pa said.

George just stood there staring. For once he didn't have anything to say, not even an important announcement.

Monster Firecracker

A dull person is one who always does what others do.

It was big, red and expensive. My brother Don had gotten it from a friend and paid him a quarter for it. A lot of money for one firecracker. But what a firecracker! It was more than four inches long, as big around as a small piece of oak firewood, and it had a fuse as long as a night crawler. Everyone knew that the longer the fuse the more powerful the firecracker.

The Fourth of July was coming up fast, and Don still didn't know where he would set off this giant of all firecrackers. He didn't want to waste it by sticking it under a tin can and seeing how far the can would fly. That was for run-of-the-mill firecrackers that were much smaller. He didn't want to stuff it in a hornet's nest and watch the hornets scatter. That was fun but way too difficult. Somebody always got stung during the stuffing. Maybe setting it off at Silver Lake, where everyone gathered for a picnic, would be appropriate. A crowd would hear it and marvel at its loud noise and impressive power. This was certainly a possibility. But there had to be a more creative use for this most powerful of Fourth of July explosives.

We hadn't yet devised a plan and here it was, the Fourth of July. We had the afternoon off from farm work and could go swimming at Silver Lake. We all piled into Pa's mostly new 1950 Chevrolet

133

with a shifting lever on the steering wheel and wonderfully fine seat cushions that still had that new-car smell, if you got your nose down real close.

"You got the firecracker?" I asked my brother Don, who was driving.

"I have," he replied. Don placed the red cylinder, that giant of all firecrackers, on the seat between us, and we were on our way to the lake. We no more than got down the driveway when Don said, "I've got it!"

"What's that?" Darrel, who sat in the backseat, asked.

"What we can do with this." He held up the red firecracker with his right hand. The great long fuse flopped back and forth.

"Let's drive by Mrs. Rapp's place."

I immediately knew what he had in mind. Mrs. Rapp was a woman without humor. To her, life was a serious matter. A kid did something a little bit wrong, at least in her eyes, and she was on the phone to her friend gabbing about it. It

> *There are those who have nothing to do but do it exceeding well.*

was the perfect use for the big red firecracker—set off Mrs. Rapp. We'd toss it on her lawn while we drove by, then stop down the road and listen to the explosion and see how she'd react. This was the plan, and a wonderful plan it was.

"What if she sees our car?" Darrel asked, concerned that she'd recognize our shiny Chevy.

"She won't see it. She'll be back in her kitchen, and by the time the firecracker goes off, we'll be well past her place," Don said.

"Sounds good to me," I said, anticipating her reaction to this most wonderful of Fourth of July pranks.

As we approached Rapp's farm, Don said, "Light the fuse." I struck a match, lit the long fuse and handed firecracker back to Don. The fuse sputtered and spit and quickly grew short.

"Throw it," Darrel yelled. And at that moment Don did.

Unfortunately, the wind caught the big cracker and blew it back into the car. It landed on the backseat by Darrel. There was no fuse left; a thin shaft of smoke shot from the fuse end of the red menace. Thinking quickly, Darrel grabbed a blanket that was always in the backseat and tossed it over the firecracker.

"Ka-bang!" It was the loudest noise I'd ever heard. The car immediately filled with a dense black smoke because both the blanket and the seat caught fire. Darrel and I beat out the fire and slowly the smoke cleared from inside the car.

My ears rang so I could scarcely hear Don yelling, "What happened?"
We drove down the road a half-mile or so and he stopped. We all got out and stood looking at each other. Darrel and I were covered with soot.

"That was some firecracker," Don said. We all agreed that it was. Then we all laughed, until

Don said, "What are we gonna tell Pa?"

Upon closer inspection, we noticed a big burned hole in the blanket. But worse, there was a burned hole in the fancy car seat. We figured we could replace the blanket, but the burned seat was another matter.

We drove around for an hour with all the windows open, to get the stink out of the car. When we got home, I rummaged around and found a blanket in my closet that looked a lot like the one we destroyed. That blanket had a new use from that day forward. It was always over the hole in the backseat.

As the days passed, Pa and Ma seemed none the wiser for our backfired prank. Maybe because whenever Pa suggested it was time to clean the car, we always volunteered without hesitation.

Hardball Tryouts

When it's over, it's often not over, except when it is.

It was my first day in high school, and John Zubeck said I should try out for the baseball team. "It's the thing to do," he said. I'd played softball at Chain O' Lake country school since first grade, and I'd gotten pretty good at it. From time to time I was even able to send the softball over the schoolyard fence, not every time at bat, but often enough that my schoolmates were impressed.

John Zubeck was a year ahead of me at Chain O' Lake. Now he was a sophomore in high school but willing to show me the ropes, to get me started on my first day there.

John met me when I crawled off the red and white school bus that sunny Monday morning in September. I was feeling a little woozy after traipsing all over the countryside picking up kids, bouncing over rough gravel roads, bending around steep turns, chasing up long hills and roaring along the flat stretches. Our farm was only four and half miles from town, but I'd bet we'd traveled thirty miles, maybe more, before we pulled up in front of the school. Some little kid, a first grader I guessed, stepped off the bus, staggered a few steps and threw up. I felt sorry for him, but watching him retch sure didn't make me feel any better.

John Zubeck was standing off to the side, waving his arm to catch my attention. "I found out

137

baseball tryouts are this afternoon," he said. Last thing I wanted to hear about was baseball. I was trying hard to keep my breakfast in place. Besides that, we never called it baseball. It was hardball at Chain O' Lake, and we didn't play it because none of us could afford the gloves that were required.

"I'll show you around," John said. It was sure nice of him. I'd heard that high school students treated the freshmen like dirt, and that's what I expected. But John was a neighbor boy and I figured he'd catch it from his ma if she found out he didn't help me out on my first day of high school.

John took me to the basement where the toilets were located. What a sight. Here was a row of white porcelain things lined up against the wall.

"Here's where you go for number one," he said. "For number two, you go in one of those stalls, shut the door, do your job and be sure and flush." Believe me, this was sure different from our two-hole outhouse at home. Here at the high school they even had toilet paper, no Sears catalogs. John showed me how to flush the toilets. I jumped back when he did it because I thought water was going to gush out all over the floor, but it didn't.

I was impressed with all that John Zubeck had learned since he got to high school. He knew what all of this stuff in the toilet room was, and he even knew how to operate it. "Be sure to wash your hands here in the sink," he said.

After the toilet tour, he showed me the gym, a great big room with a fancy, shiny wood floor and basketball hoops on each end. There was a basketball in the corner, and he tossed it to me. This was the first time I'd ever seen or touched a basketball.

I paid close attention to everything John told me because I knew that after today I'd be on my own. My guess was that come tomorrow, he'd hardly know who I was. I learned that juniors and seniors, and particularly sophomores, wanted nothing whatsoever to do with freshmen, espe-

Avoid sticking your hand in a dark hole.

cially those that came off the farm. I'd start worrying about all that tomorrow. First I had to get through today.

It was time for classes to start, and John showed me where my first one was. He said he'd meet me for lunch, and he pointed to where the lunchroom was located.

I sat in my math class and noticed that there were at least twenty other kids there, too. The only one I knew was Kenny Owens, and he sat in the back with students I surmised were town kids. He lived on a farm but had always gone to town school, so he considered himself one of them. He did look up and give me a halfhearted wave when I came into the room. I gave him credit for that.

Before I knew it, it was lunchtime, and I made my way down the stairs for the lunch hall. The closer I got the stronger the smell of sauerkraut. No problem finding the lunch hall: just follow your nose.

"Ready for baseball tryouts?" John said when he saw me. I hadn't given baseball a thought. My mind was such a clutter of arithmetic, social stud-

ies, history, and the rules for this and that I'd forgotten how hungry I was. And I'd completely forgotten about baseball tryouts.

I got in line and soon I found a big pile of smelly, stringy, steaming sauerkraut on my plate, with a shriveled-up wiener parked on top. It was a sorrowful sight, and I immediately thought about the little kid from the bus with the upset stomach and how he must have felt when he confronted his lunch of sauerkraut and shriveled wiener. I swallowed hard and dug in. We had sauerkraut at home every so often, but Ma sure knew how to fix it better than the cook here.

"Here's what you do, Jerry, when it's your turn to bat," John said. He was bound and determined to get me ready for baseball tryouts. "You hold the bat just like in softball and you stand right up to the plate and stare down the pitcher," he said.

I was trying to listen and eat at the same time. The smell of sauerkraut in the room was overpowering. I was only half hearing what John had to say.

The afternoon slipped by just as fast as the

morning, and soon I was standing in line with several other freshmen, trying out for the baseball team. I didn't tell anybody that this was the first time I'd ever played baseball. I also didn't tell the coach or the other kids that I'd had polio the previous winter and wasn't able to move very fast. The only thing I knew for sure was I wanted to get on the baseball team.

"You'll just never amount to nothin' in high school if you're not on the baseball team," John Zubeck had said. He had gotten on the team last year and played somewhere in the outfield. Left field, he told me. I looked out in the field, and there he was, way out there. If you'd asked me where John played I'd have said, "left out," but that wouldn't have been very nice.

Finally, it was my turn to step up to the plate and take a few swings at the ball like the other boys were doing. Some of these guys were good. David Jones, the kid in front of me, hit the first ball pitched to him and it flew right over the head of the second baseman. You hit a hardball square on and it really sails, goes a whole bunch further than a softball.

I tried to remember what John Zubeck had said about holding the bat and standing up to the plate and staring down the pitcher. The pitcher was Cliff Simonson, and he was good. He could whistle that ball across the plate so hard that the dust flew when it hit the catcher's mitt. Marty Inda was catcher, a tall kid with long arms and the blackest hair.

"You ready?" Simonson yelled at me.

"I am," I said. I tried to sound confident, but I'm sure my voice sounded like some scared little farm kid who'd never played baseball before. I hardly saw the ball fly past me. Ka-whap. Marty had the ball in his hand, and he came up and showed it to me. I don't know why he did that. I knew what a baseball looked like.

I shuffled a little closer to the plate, stared down the pitcher and got myself ready again.

The next thing I remember I was on the

> *Slow down.*

ground, in the dust by home plate, and everyone was looking down at me. Kind of a dumb feeling to see all those faces staring down at you. The coach asked if I was all right. I had a notion to say that if I was all right I wouldn't be laid out here in the dirt. But I didn't say anything. Cliff Simonson and Marty Inda lifted me to my feet, and I staggered around a little, trying to get my bearings. My head felt awful. I reached up and found a huge lump just above my left eye.

The coach took me aside. "Apps, you don't move fast enough to play baseball." I looked at him and didn't say anything. I wanted to tell him about my having had polio but thought better of it. Pa always said, "Don't make excuses; it usually doesn't help."

I'm sure I had one of the shortest baseball careers in the history of the game—just two pitches and that was it. It was all over.

PART III
Farm Talk

A Glossary

Neighbor fellow talked so loud that nobody could hear him.

Acts like he owns the place.
Used in a variety of ways to describe someone or something that behaves in a high-and-mighty manner. "That homely cow is so bossy, she acts like she owns the place."

Afoot or horseback.
A state of confusion. "Billy B. doesn't know if he's afoot or horseback, but then he's always been confused."

Ainso.
Usually spoken at the end of a statement, as in "Cold winter we're having, ainso?"

Air is close.
A phrase used to describe a high-humidity day. "Air is so close today it feels like it's a hundred degrees."

All worked up.
Irritable about something. "Ethel's all worked up because Mable's pie got first prize at the fair, and she only got second."

At the end of his rope.
When someone is out of options. "Last week's hailstorm ruined his corn crop and George is at the end of his rope."

Axed the deal.
The bargain is off. "Joe ordered ten bushels of rutabagas, but his wife Edith axed the deal."

Aye, yes or no.
When a person is expected to say something but doesn't. "Clyde stomped out of church without saying aye, yes or no."

Babe is born.
When a difficult job has been completed. "The babe is born! Thought we'd never get the fence strung across that hollow."

Bad one.
When something goes wrong or something unexpected happens. Farmer might say, "Never saw it rain so hard this time of year; it's a bad one."

Barking up the wrong tree.
Making a wrong decision or wrongly accusing someone. "Paul's barking up the wrong tree. Emil had nothing to do with swiping his watermelons."

Battle-ax.
A rather impolite way of describing a woman not well liked. "She's an old battle-ax—don't cross her path if you don't have to."

Beat around the bush.
Avoid getting to the point. "That Sigrud beats around the bush and never gets around to telling you what he thinks."

Bee in her bonnet.
Agitated about something. "Norma sure had a bee in her bonnet about the new preacher."

Beeline.
Going straight toward some goal, as a honeybee might do. "She made a beeline to the yard goods at the mercantile."

Bent out of shape.
See "Pickled."

Blind as a bat.
Usually spoken when someone overlooks something that is right in front of him. "You're as blind as a bat—that buck wasn't twenty yards away."

Blow out the lamp.
What you said to the last person to go to bed, before you had electricity. "When you finish reading, Herm, be sure and blow out the lamp."

Born in the barn.
Used to describe someone lacking in manners or social graces. "Close the door when you come in the house! You'd think you were born in the barn."

Brand-new.
Something that has never been used. Farm kids didn't see many brand-new things, except for overalls, long underwear, and six-buckle overshoes. "All the kids crowded around Mildred's shiny, brand-new bike."

Broad side of a barn.
Usually referred to a hunter who couldn't shoot straight. "He can't hit the broad side of a barn; he'll never get a deer this season."

Bushed.
Tired. Worn out. Ready to sit down. "I've been splitting wood all day and I'm bushed."

Can't cut the mustard.
Not up to the job. "That new fella from the city will never be a farmer, he just can't cut the mustard."

Cat's meow.
When someone thinks highly of himself. "Look at Joe strutting around in his new boots, thinking he's the cat's meow."

Changed its tune.
When someone decides to do something that they previously refused to do. "The power company changed its tune about signing up farmers when the REA came into the county."

Chew the fat.
When two or more people are talking. Generally what men do when they gather around the woodstove in the back of the hardware store. "What were you doing in town, George?" Irene asked. "Just chewing the fat," he said, grinning.

Clean as a whistle.
When something is absolutely clean. "That stove top is clean as a whistle—not a speck of grime anywhere."

Cobbled up.
Patching something together so that it works, barely. "Henry's tractor was so cobbled up you'd wonder why it ran at all."

Comical.
When something unusual occurs. May or may not be humorous. "You should see what Joe's cows did to Emil's cornfield. It was comical."

Cracking the whip.
Being in charge. Calling out orders. "Felix is a tough guy to work for; he's always cracking the whip."

Crooked as a snake.
Dishonest. "That salesman is crooked as a snake—he'd cheat you as soon as look at you."

Crow.
To brag. "Bill's been crowing about his big corn crop."

Crust of bread.
Said when a relative stops by at mealtime. "Why don't you stay for supper? I think we've still got a crust of bread."

Dandy.
When something is special—larger than normal, faster than usual—and someone is glad to have it. "See that big bay horse, isn't she a dandy?"

Davenport.
A sofa found in the parlor and used only for special occasions. Was always kept looking nice. "Danny, get off the davenport, the preacher is coming this afternoon."

Dead as a doornail.
Very dead. "We tried to save the old sow, but she was dead as a doornail."

Dead horse.
The issue is closed. "I don't wanna to talk anymore about last Saturday night. It's a dead horse."

Dicker.
Bargain, negotiate. "Pa's been dickering with the cow buyer for more than an hour."

Dish to pass.
A casserole, salad, bowl of Jell-O, baked beans or meat-balls—brought to a potluck dinner at the country school, or a church gathering. "Ma always made a tuna casserole for the dish to pass at the church social."

Doesn't give a damn.
Not caring, unconcerned. "Floyd doesn't give a damn what happens to his hay crop."

Doesn't have a prayer.
What is said when someone tries something that can't be done. "Jim Kolka wants to drive his old car all the way to Appleton. He doesn't have a prayer."

Doesn't know beans when the bag is open.
Stupid, ignorant. "That new hired man is so dumb he doesn't know beans when the bag is open."

Dog tired.
See "Bushed."

Don't fuss.
Said when you accept an invitation to have supper at the neighbors' and don't expect anything special. "We'd love to come, but don't fuss now, Lorraine."

Don't let go of something until you got hold of something else.
Good advice for planning next year's crops, dealing with

your banker, and being civil toward your wife. "Hear you're thinking about hiring out to another farmer. Just remember, don't let go of something until you got hold of something else."

Dumb as an ox.
Usually refers to someone who can't seem to do a job properly, such as digging potatoes or chopping wood. "Poor old Ernie is as dumb as an ox—he thought that if he fed his chickens twice as much, they'd give twice as many eggs."

Dumb cluck.
Words used to describe someone who has made a mistake or probably many of them. "Gad, he is such a dumb cluck he doesn't know enough to come in outta the rain."

Euchred.
Comes from the card game euchre (you-ker) that is played in many rural communities. To be euchred is to get something less than you expect. "George was euchred when he bought that lame horse at Fred's auction."

Face that would stop a clock.
A description of a homely person. "Jane wouldn't win any beauty contests; she had a face that would stop a clock."

Flew the coop.
Leaving without warning. "Hear about the new school-marm? She flew the coop without telling a soul."

Full of wind.
Said when someone talked a lot but didn't say anything. Politicians come to mind. "That candidate makes big promises, but he's just full of wind."

Funny thing.
When something unusual or unexplainable happens. Person observing may say, "It's a funny thing. Don't know how that happened."

Fuss over.
Spending undue time with something. "Agnes makes such a fuss over baking a cake for the church social."

Get your goat.
When someone says something that antagonizes you. "I just can't stand being around Ethel; she knows how to get my goat."

Give him his head.
Letting someone do a job the way he wants. Comes from relaxing the reins on a horse. "Give Fred his head on this, Pa, he knows what he's doing."

Go fly a kite.
An order to leave, usually spoken in disgust. "If you can't

do the work, then go fly a kite."

Gone haywire.
When something breaks. "My old tractor has gone haywire again."

Gone to the dogs.
Sinking to a new low. "Would you look at Smith's farm! It's really gone to the dogs."

Grip.
Old-fashioned name for a suitcase. "Ma took her grip and went off to visit her sister in town."

Grippe.
The flu. "Poor Ethyl has to do the chores. Mac has been in bed with the grippe for two weeks."

Had a snootful.
See "Pickled."

Hard row to hoe.
A difficult job or situation. "Joe's barn burned last week. He'll have a hard row to hoe until he builds a new one."

Having a bird.
Being agitated. "Mable's having a bird because it's been raining every day, and she can't air out her rugs."

Haywire together.
Patch something up so that it will work, at least in the short run. "Joe'll haywire together that old grain binder and cut as much grain as if he had a new one."

Head over teakettle.
Falling down, usually head first. "Did you see Joe go head over teakettle when he stepped in that hole?"

Hemming and hawing.
Not able to make up your mind. "There's Floyd, hemming and hawing. He can never decide on anything."

Hey dere.
A form of greeting in some rural communities, something like "Hi" but with more meaning and feeling. "Hey dere, Morty, good ta see ya."

Hide nor hair.
When someone or some thing is lost without a trace. "Hear about Justin's horse running away? He can't find hide nor hair of it." Also, to define a confusing situation— "I can't make hide nor hair out of what that guy is saying."

High on the hog.
Having folks think you're living right up there with the

rich people. "Look at old Amos, he's living high on the hog since he started drawing Social Security."

High pockets.
Used to describe a man who is tall. "High pockets Smith can pick apples without a ladder."

High water pants.
Pants that are too short and come halfway up the ankle. Often seen on teenage boys. "Frank's boy really grew this summer. Look at those high water pants."

His tail is draggin'.
A description of someone who has a spent a long day making hay, picking cucumbers, or doing a hundred other farm jobs. See "Bushed."

Hit the nail on the head.
To get it right. "That Joe, he hits the nail on the head every time. He always knows how to solve the problem."

Hit the road.
Leave right now. "It's getting late. Time we hit the road."

Hold your horses.
Spoken to someone in a hurry. "Hold your horses, Ethyl, I'm coming."

Homely as sin.
Can't be much more unattractive. See "Face that would stop a clock."

Hope in hell.
When someone doesn't have a chance to succeed at something. "Oscar doesn't have a hope in hell for getting in his hay before it rains."

Hound dog look.
How a person looks when everything has gone wrong. "John's had a hound dog look since his best cow died."

In a pickle.
In a difficult situation. "Adolph's in a pickle. He can't even make the interest payment on his mortgage."

Into a fix.
Finding oneself in some difficulty. Similar to "In a pickle." "She's gotten into a fix now that her car has slid off the road."

Jell-O.
A food that has multiple uses by farm families. With some shredded carrots in it, it's a salad. With bananas and a dab of whipped cream, it becomes dessert. On special occasions, it is molded into shapes varying from turkeys to

stars to Christmas trees. Always served at church suppers, weddings and funerals so that some see it having religious qualities. A first question often asked when planning a potluck: "Who's bringing the Jell-O?"

Jumped over the traces.
What a horse did when it stepped over a tug and got tangled in its harness. What a young man did on Saturday night that he shouldn't have. "Hear about young Ben Hansen? He's gone and jumped over the traces again. Drove home skunk drunk and ran his car into a tree."

Just down the road.
Phrase used in giving directions. May mean around the corner; may also mean five miles away. "Drive until you cross the creek, then turn right and keep going until you come to a big cow pasture where you turn left. Keep driving and you'll spot Emil's place on the right. It's just down the road."

Just like uptown.
Fixing up something so that it's special. "The new concrete floor in the barn is just like uptown."

Keep your shirt on.
Be patient. Wait a little. Don't get excited. "Keep your shirt on, Mable. I'll have the mice out of the pantry before you know it."

Laying down on the job.
Shirking a duty or not completing a task. "We'll never get that field of potatoes dug if Weston keeps laying down on the job."

Let the cat out of the bag.
Prematurely divulging a secret. "For heaven's sake, Paul, don't let the cat out of the bag. We don't want everyone to know the schoolmarm is pregnant."

Lickety-split.
Very quickly. "The kids came lickety-split when they smelled cookies hot out of the oven."

Lied like a rug.
Not known to be truthful. "When asked her age, Agnes lied like a rug."

Like a bat out of hell.
Faster than "Lickety-split."

Like a chicken with its head cut off.
A person who runs hither and yon with no apparent direction. "Marge is so panicked about organizing the church picnic she's acting like a chicken with its head cut off."

Limp as a dishrag.
Not stiff. For instance, when carrying a sleeping child, the mother might say, "Joey is as limp as a dishrag."

Long underwear.
A cold-weather garment worn under clothes by nearly all farmers in winter. Some wear it in summer, too, proclaiming, "What keeps the heat in keeps the heat out."

Lunch.
Usually served in mid-morning, mid-afternoon, or in the evening when neighbors come by to play cards. Consists of bologna sandwiches, Jell-O, sliced cheese, at least two kinds of cake, cookies and lots of coffee. "Always like to play cards at Sorenson's, 'cause Mable makes the best lunch."

Make a stink.
When someone disagrees with something that happens or some decision that is made. "John sure can make a stink when things don't go his way."

Make hay while the sun shines.
Getting something done when the conditions are right. "Let's haul those pigs to market while the prices are up. Gotta make hay while the sun shines."

Meat-and-potatoes guy.
An average fellow who doesn't go for surprises whether they be exotic food, wild women or fast cars. "My George doesn't want anything fancy. He's a meat-and-potatoes guy."

Nailed down.
Something difficult is figured out. "Fred couldn't decide for the longest time what he should plant on that low ground down by the creek. Finally he's got it nailed down."

Neck of the woods.
Refers to a particular geographic area. "How are things in your neck of the woods?"

New.
Describes something a person didn't have before. May be a car, horse, cow, wife or a tractor. Not to be confused with "Brand-new." "I finally got me a new horse. He's only ten years old."

No power in it.
A reference to bland, squishy store-bought bread. "Eat only homemade bread. That store-bought stuff has no power in it."

No sin to be poor.
True, but it can be mighty inconvenient at times.

Nose to the grindstone.
Working at a difficult, often tedious job. "June has had her nose to the grindstone all fall getting the house ready for the holidays."

Off his feed.
The person isn't feeling well. "Dave is off his feed. He must be coming down with the grippe."

Oh, shoot.
Uttered by Methodists or Baptists who have difficulty cussing when something goes wrong. "Oh, shoot! This old jalopy's got another flat tire."

Old bat.
Reference to a disliked older woman. "That old bat never has a good word to say about anyone."

On the fritz.
See "Gone haywire." "Oh, shoot, the milking machine is on the fritz again."

On the mend.
When someone who has been injured or ill is recovering. Could also refer to a horse or a cow. "That broken arm looked bad, but I think old Fritz is finally on the mend."

One-horse town.
A rather small place with limited resources. "Willow Creek is a one-horse town; you can't even buy a pair of overalls there."

Out tomcattin'.
What young men did (do) on Saturday nights. "You'd think those guys would grow up. They were out tomcattin' until four this morning."

Parlor.
That room in a farmhouse that was saved for city relatives' visits. In many homes, it was closed off in the winter. Also known as the front room. "Company's coming. Got to air out the parlor."

Peter out.
Stopping before a job is finished. "Bill always peters out before he gets his hay in."

Pickled.
The effect from spending too much time in the village bar. "George was so pickled last night, he fell asleep on the way home, ran into the ditch and spent the night in his car."

Pickles.
Cucumbers, beets, watermelons and assorted other vegetables that are preserved in brine. Another word for cow's teats, as in "that cow has ticklish pickles."

Pig.
Critter that digs around in the barnyard. Also a neighbor who helps himself to three servings of roast beef and accepts a second piece of pie when offered. "Paul's such a pig, he eats as much as three people."

Plowed that ground before.
When someone insists on telling you something in great detail that they have told you before. "Let's not talk about who you're gonna vote for. We've plowed that ground before."

Pouring money down a rat hole.
When something is done that turns out to be a mistake. John said, "Buying that skinny cow was just like pouring money down a rat hole."

Proud.
A horse that walks with his head high, a cow that leads the herd and a farmer who wears his cap at a jaunty angle. "See how that old brindle cow walks, she sure is proud."

Put one over.
To get the upper hand; to best someone. "Hear about that lazy horse Paul sold Clarence? Paul sure put one over on him."

Put the damper on.
Quit talking. "John, you've said enough. Put the damper on." Comes from the damper on a stovepipe, used to control the fire in a stove.

Put the lid on.
See "Put the damper on."

Putting on the dog.
Showing off, often with the kind of clothing worn. "Look at Emily with her fancy new dress. She's really putting on the dog."

Right up to snuff.
Keeping up with the neighbors. "Oscar just put a new coat of red paint on his barn and now he's right up to snuff."

Rule the roost.
To be in charge. Comes from the chicken house where the biggest, meanest rooster was in charge of all the hens. "Go to Charlie's house and you'll see who rules the roost—it's his wife, Mable."

Run for your money.
Good competition. "Joe really knows how to grow corn—he gave me a run for my money."

Runs off at the mouth.
Someone who keeps on talking…and talking. "Joe was running off at his mouth so much, I thought he'd never shut up."

Scarcer than hen's teeth.
None can be found. "Blackberries are scarcer than hen's teeth this year."

Shoot the breeze.
See "Chew the fat."

Shoot the bull.
several farmers gather to discuss important matters of the day. Others hearing the discussion may have a different opinion as to its importance. See "Chew the fat."

Shoots off his mouth.
Speak out of turn. Say things that shouldn't be said. "As often as Clyde shoots off his mouth, you'd think someone would take a swing at him."

Short end of the stick.
When people believe that they received less than they deserved. "I think I got the short end of the stick on that deal."

Shut his trap.
Words used in reference to someone who talks too much. "I wish he'd shut his trap."

Skunk drunk.
A fellow who has spent so much time in the tavern that he requires three neighbors and one irate wife to put him to bed. See "Pickled."

Sleep tight, don't let the bedbugs bite.
Affectionate nursery rhyme spoken to children when they are off to bed.

Slick as can be.
Smoothly done, without a hitch. "You see John Evans drive that big load of hay through those narrow barn doors? It was just as slick as can be."

Smell to high heaven.
Said about that which smells really bad. "Paul Johnson smells to high heaven. Bet he hasn't had a bath in weeks."

Snookered.
Cheated out of something. "I think that cow dealer snookered me, 'cause my new cow kicks anyone who gets

near her."

Snowing down south.
Said when a lady's slip is showing. "Say, Miss Thompson, better look in the mirror 'cause it's snowing down south."

So skinny he doesn't cast a shadow.
Thin. "Marge needs to fatten up her son Tommy—he's so skinny he doesn't cast a shadow."

So tight he squeaks.
Stingy. Squeezes each dollar before letting go. "Not much use asking Albert Knutson to buy a raffle ticket; he's so tight he squeaks."

So, how's the weather there?
One of the first questions asked when rural people converse with someone outside their community.

Souser.
Man who spends too much time in a tavern.

Spell.
Period of time, as in "Sit for a spell." Or when someone has a recurring symptom of some unknown illness. "She's having another one of her spells."

Spiffy.
All fancied up. "Joe's looking spiffy tonight. He's wearing

a new pair of bib overalls and has greased down his hair."

Straight with the world.
Making sure that fences, buildings, corn rows, hay cocks and grain shocks all are straight north and south, or east and west. "Look at Frank's new hay shed, he's built it absolutely straight with the world."

Strange duck.
Someone with an unusual appearance or who does unusual things. "That Joe Ames is a strange duck; he doesn't milk his cows until nine in the morning."

Sucking hind tit.
Someone who is not doing well in competition with others. Comes from little pigs suckling at their mother; the smallest one often got the last teat in a row, which usually had the least milk. "That Bill Swenson has got the poorest farm. He'll end up sucking hind tit again this year."

Take a hike.
Time to leave. "When young Oscar came by to take Fred's pretty daughter to the dance, Oscar told him to take a hike."

Take the bull by the horns.
To take charge of a situation. "Fred has taken the bull by

157

the horns and decided to fix the roof on his barn."

Takes the cake.
When someone does something special. "Little Susie won the spelling bee at school. Doesn't that just take the cake?"

Taking over the home farm.
Going back to work on the farm after several misguided years in the city. "Ralph's moving back from Chicago to take over the home farm."

Tall drink of water.
Someone who is taller than normal. "Have you seen that Jimmy Davis lately? He's sure a tall drink of water."

Thunder bucket.
Slop jar stored under the bed for nighttime emergencies. "The worst chore on the farm was emptying the thunder buckets."

Thunderstruck.
Astonished. "He was thunderstruck when the load of hay tipped over."

Too big for his britches.
Someone filled with self-importance. "That Billy Johnson is so cocky, he's too big for his britches."

Too many cooks spoil the broth.
Words used to keep your mother-in-law out of the kitchen.

Took the bit in his mouth.
When someone takes on a hard job. "Somebody had to tell George that lightning killed three of his cows. Fred took the bit in his mouth and did it."

Tough as nails.
Being able to continue on a difficult job beyond expectations. "She's tough as nails. Look how she handles that three-tine fork."

Tough as shoe leather.
A description of meat that is difficult to chew. "That roast sure looked good, but it was as tough as shoe leather."

Truth.
A term used to describe something that storytellers believe shouldn't be contaminated with facts. "Don't listen for any facts in Paul's stories; I don't think there's one thing accurate when he says it's the truth."

Two ax handles wide.
A not very polite way of describing the backside of a plump woman. "Laverne has a lovely face, but her backside is two ax handles wide."

Two shakes of a lamb's tail.
The job will be finished in short order. "I'll be finished milking this cow in two shakes of a lamb's tail."

Two-fisted drinker.
A big fellow who can handle his drink—usually. "Dave's moving slow today—he was out with Frank, that two-fisted drinker, last night."

Under the weather.
Not feeling well. "Mable, you'll have to do the milking tonight; I'm a little under the weather."

Until the cows come home.
Waiting a long time for something to happen. "If you wait for the price of corn to come up, you'll wait until the cows come home."

Up a tree.
Caught not knowing which way to turn. "Bill is up a tree. He doesn't know if he should sell the cow that gives the most milk even though she kicks him every chance she gets."

Walking a little short.
May refer to an old horse, an old dog, an old cow, or an old farmer who can't quite move as fast as he once did. "Haven't seen Paul Evans for nearly a year. He's walking a little short isn't he?"

Weak-kneed.
A person not up to lifting more than fifty pounds or so. "I wouldn't hire Allen Collins to load potato sacks, if I were you. He's about the most weak-kneed guy in the village."

Wet rain.
The kind that falls lightly but soaks you nonetheless. "Didn't seem like much moisture was coming down, but it turned out to be a wet rain and I was soaked to the skin."

What's going around.
Usually refers to a cold or a flu that others in the neighborhood have gotten. "I'm not feeling well. Got what's going around."

Whistle another tune.
When someone changes his mind. "George said he'd never raise hogs, then the price went way up and he started to whistle another tune. Said he was buying fifty."

Windbag.
See "Full of wind."

Windy.
Someone who tends to exaggerate. "Your Uncle Ellsworth is a bit on the windy order, I'd say."

Woodpecker thaw.
A few days of warm weather in midwinter, usually February, when the barn roof eaves drip, the snow becomes mushy, and ponds form in the hollows. Likely comes from seeing birds actively eating during a warm spell in winter, especially woodpeckers. "Them new neighbors from the south actually thought this was an early spring, but I told 'em it's just a woodpecker thaw."

Works like a horse.
A description of someone who is a hard worker. "Jim's got himself a good wife; she works like a horse."

Worn to a frazzle.
Tired out. Not able to do much else before resting. "I'm afraid I'll have to miss the church social; I'm worn to a frazzle."

You can just come to hell.
Spoken in a fit of anger by someone who has difficulty keeping his verbs straight, or is looking for a companion to join him where he already believes he is. When angry at someone, Joe Jensen would shake his finger and say, "You can just come to hell."

Your barn door is open.
Zip up your pants.

Youse guys.
When more than two people are assembled. "So what do youse guys wanna do, go hunting squirrels or play softball?"

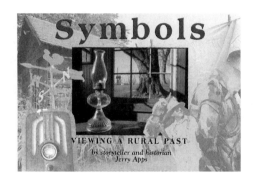

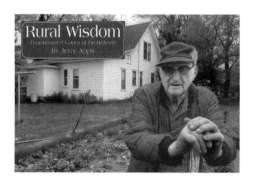